CW00553954

WILD swimming

Torbay

Adventures on Devon's Riviera

Matt Newbury & Sophie Pierce
Underwater photography by Dan Bolt

WILD THINGS PUBLISHING

"Poets have sung of the beauties of Torbay, some of the greatest of English novelists have woven romances on its shores, monarchs and diplomats have likened it to the Bay of Naples and the lagoons of the Southern Seas. Torbay is always impressively beautiful, whether it be seen on a bright calm day in summer, when its surface shimmers and sparkles like a million deep blue sapphires; or on an autumn night, when the harvest moon creates a pathway of red-gold upon it; or in winter, when the white horses chase each other to its shores." 1925 Tourist Guide

WILD swimming
Torbay

"For the swimmers, the bathers,
the slippers and sliders
The floaters, the drifters,
the duckers and divers
The waders. the plungers,
the splashers and gliders
Skinny dippers, strokers,
doggie paddlers, freestylers.

Come on in, the water waits"

CONTENTS

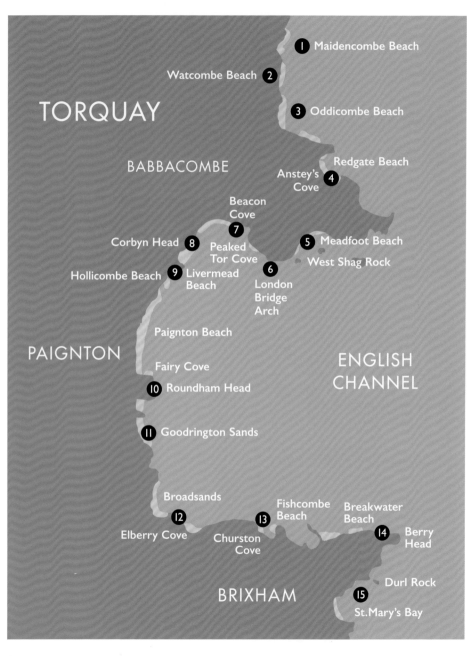

TORQUAY

BABBACOMBE

1 Maidencombe Beach

Watcombe Beach 2

3 Oddicombe Beach

Redgate Beach

Anstey's Cove 4

Beacon Cove

7

Corbyn Head 8

5 Meadfoot Beach

Peaked Tor Cove

West Shag Rock

Hollicombe Beach 9

Livermead Beach

6

London Bridge Arch

Paignton Beach

PAIGNTON

Fairy Cove

ENGLISH CHANNEL

10 Roundham Head

11 Goodrington Sands

Broadsands

12

Elberry Cove

Churston Cove

13 Fishcombe Beach

Breakwater Beach

14 Berry Head

Durl Rock

BRIXHAM

15 St.Mary's Bay

THE LOCATIONS

FOREWORD

A decade has passed since we first wrote this book, and, goodness, what a lot has changed. Back then, swimming outdoors, particularly in the winter, usually attracted bewildered (and sometimes disapproving) looks and the 'are you mad?' response. Now, it seems, everyone is doing it, as people are realising how good it makes you feel. When you swim, you undergo a kind of transformation, and when you come out of the water, you feel changed for the better.

One of the main motivations for originally writing the book was to convey the unspoilt beauty of the Torbay coast, which can easily be explored by swimming 'beyond the beach', as we put it back then. We knew, from our own explorations, that the shoreline contained many fascinating caves, cliffs, rock formations and lagoons, but that many people didn't get to see them, as they never swam away from the main beaches. We put together a list of swim journeys, which we published, along with a series of stunning images by our friend, underwater photographer Dan Bolt.

Ten years on, these hidden gems are still as beautiful, and with so many more people falling in love with swimming, it feels like the right time to republish the book. We've given it a new name, *Wild Swimming Torbay*, and a new look, and added more information. We owe huge thanks to our publisher, Daniel Start, who has brought the book to life again.

Matt Newbury and Sophie Pierce, Spring 2023

INTRODUCTION

*T*hink of wild places, and you don't tend to think of Torbay. You might think of the rugged, empty coast of Cornwall, or maybe Dartmoor or the untamed shores of Wales; places without people. But the populated seaside resorts of Torquay, Paignton and Brixham, with their deck chairs, hotels, holiday parks and ice cream vans? Surely not?

Well, think again. Torbay has a secret, wild, side, with untold natural beauty. To experience it, all you have to do is get in the water and swim. Seen from the sea, Torbay's coastline is transformed. It's a bit like stepping into a wardrobe and coming out in Narnia; a new world reveals itself, with azure, gin-clear sea, and mysterious caves, islands and rock formations.

Torbay has a huge advantage over many of Great Britain's other beautiful swimming locations, because its waters are very safe. It's a natural harbour, and so the sea is shallow, there are hardly any currents, and the water tends to be flat, calm and beautifully blue. Because the entrance to the Bay faces east, it is also sheltered from the prevailing south westerly winds. It has a wonderfully varied array of beaches and settings, from the red sands and cliffs of Paignton, to the dramatic islands off Hope's Nose, limestone caves near Berry Head, and the terracotta cliffs and rocky outcrops of Watcombe and Maidencombe.

Generations have found Torbay the perfect place to swim; indeed, in the past, Torbay had what could be described as a 'golden age' of swimming, which began when people first discovered the health benefits of a dip in the sea. In 1900, renowned cliff diver Tack Collins (pictured on page 15) thrilled people with daring stunt diving from Saddle Rock in Torquay. Swim clubs had hundreds of members, the more adventurous of whom would think nothing of swimming miles out to a ship when the fleet was in, to be given a tot of rum as a reward for their endeavour.

SOME HISTORY

The health benefits of sea swimming were first recognised by the ancient Greeks. More recently, the concept of seaside resorts as places of recuperation can probably be traced to an 18th century physician called Dr Richard Russell, who wrote a book with the charming title of *Glandular Consumption and the uses of Seawater in the Treatment of the Glands*. Such was the popularity of his writing, seaside health spas started to spring up across the coast, with bathing machines adding colour and excitement to beaches.

Various other publications tried to identify watering places that were especially good for the treatment of specific diseases. In 1842, a highly respected doctor from Exeter called Thomas Shapter wrote a treatise called *The Climate of the South of Devon and*

The Marine Spa, Torquay, 1920s

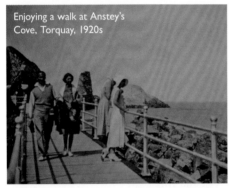

Enjoying a walk at Anstey's Cove, Torquay, 1920s

A packed Torre Abbey Sands, Torquay, 1920s

its Influence upon Health. He recommended Sidmouth's mild air to "consumptives" and those suffering from "overwrought intellect", while Exmouth's bracing winds were said to be perfect for those with "weakly children" and those with questionable morals. Torquay and Dawlish, the author claimed, were "suitable during the winter to persons labouring under chest complaints". He even went so far as to claim that Teignmouth's agreeable climate was ideally suited for restoring the health and strength "of those who may have suffered from the climates of the East of West Indies."

People started travelling down to Torquay, believing the climate and sea air would assist their recovery from various illnesses. On Beacon Cove, what is now the Regina Hotel was the home of the original Torquay Medical Baths, where those not well enough to brave the sea could visit premises opened by a Mr Pollard to endure hot, tepid, vapour, shower and cold seawater baths. The poet Elizabeth Barrett was a patient there in 1840. However, having so many sick people in one place tended to cause the various illnesses to spread further. That same year, Dr A B Granville wrote about the new wellness industry, saying:

"The Frying Pan along the Strand is filled with respirator-bearing people who look like muzzled ghosts, and ugly enough to frighten the younger people to death". Torquay was "the south west asylum for diseased lungs", with the hotels "filled with spitting pots and echoing to the sounds of cavernous coughs; outside the only sound to be heard was the frequent tolling of the funeral bell."

Towards the end of the 19th century, efforts were made to reverse this trend, and try and attract tourists, rather than invalids. 1902 saw the first advertising campaign to market Torquay to summer tourists and the resort was branded 'Queen of the Watering Places'. The rapidly expanding resort adopted the motto 'Salus et Felicitas' or 'health and happiness.' It's an appropriate slogan, which can still be spotted on buildings like Torquay Town Hall and The Pavilion.

As part of the new tourism boom, people started taking to the waters and a series of segregated beaches opened. The growth in the popularity of swimming coincided with a change in attitudes, and mixed bathing was finally allowed in 1900, thanks to the efforts of one Ernest Hutchings, who later became the Torquay Coroner. By this time beaches were packed with people swimming both competitively and for fun, and old postcards show people squashed like sardines on the beaches of Torquay, Paignton and Brixham.

Towards the end of the twentieth century, with the growth of cheap flights and package holidays, people seemed to fall out of love with swimming in British waters. Fortunately, the popularity of sea swimming once again seems to be on the rise. What, perhaps, some don't realise, is quite how many exciting aquatic journeys you can experience in this beautiful part of Devon. And that's what this book is all about. We want to take you on explorations by water; Torbay has so many amazing sights to see from the sea.

Take London Bridge for example (pictured

Tack Collins diving from Saddle Rock in 1900

on page 17). This is a stunning natural rock arch just a few hundred metres along the coast from the Imperial Hotel. It's right in the centre of Torquay, but because of its position – only accessible from the water – many people don't realise it's there. But if you're prepared to get in the water, it's a short swim away.

One of the most appealing things about swimming in the sea is the feeling of going on an adventure along the coastline. There is so much to experience, from the natural flora and fauna, through the history of man's activities on the coast, and the unusual geology which forms the shoreline itself.

GEOLOGICAL ADVENTURES

As swimmers, the rocks around us form the most evocative backdrop, creating atmospheres ranging from high drama through to mystery and intrigue. But how often do we stop to wonder what the rocks are telling us about the formation of the earth itself? And what life was like millions of years ago? The geology of Torbay is fascinating, telling a compelling story about life on earth so long ago that one can barely imagine it, and the best place to see it is from the sea.

Swimming along the shore you can see evidence of three main periods of geological history - the Devonian, Carboniferous and Permian. It all started just over four and half billion years ago when the earth wasn't actually here; there were just hot gases and rocks spinning around in space, which eventually formed the earth. Over millions of years cells evolved, and so started the beginnings of life.

The first period we really see in Torbay, the Devonian, was around 400 million years ago. Torbay was a shallow, tropical sea, with lots of marine wildlife. Devonian limestone can be seen mostly at the northern and southern ends of the Bay, at Torquay and Brixham, and it was formed from an ancient tropical reef built mostly of hard sponges but also early corals and a wealth of exotic life now extinct. Layer upon layer these creatures accumulated on the seabed and were later compressed over millions of years by younger sediments on top to form hard limestone.

The wealth of creatures were slowly fossilised as minerals carried by water crystallised to replace the hard parts of that once ancient life to form natural solid rock replicas. These fossilised remains are today visible in lots of places in Torbay, forming beautiful abstract patterns in the rocks. In many places they still actually look like corals; you can spot these formations at Elberry Cove near Churston, and at both Oddicombe and Meadfoot in Torquay, to name just a few places.

After the Devonian period came the Carboniferous period, between 300 and 350 million years ago. It was a time of great instability, with the earth's tectonic plates shifting around. Along the coast of Torbay, you can frequently see great folds in the rock, notably at the London Bridge arch, where immense pressure movement happened and these rocks were trapped deep under massive mountains that were formed. In some places the rocks were turned completely upside down.

After this, the land mass of which Torbay was part moved northwards, and landlocked, it became a dry desert, like the Sahara is today. This was the Permian period, which was between 300 and 250 million years ago. Torbay was between 15 and 30 degrees north of the equator and was incredibly hot. There were extreme storms which caused flash-floods in the mountains, sweeping stones and rocks down onto the plains below where the water rapidly sank into the parched and rocky ground.

At this time the Bay was covered by these desert rocks, some of them sand dunes and

some of them rock debris, called Breccia, many of which are apparent in the red rocks around Paignton. Much later oxidation of the irons in the rocks turned them red and this is what gives the so-called Permian red rock of Torbay its distinctive colour.

Such is the significance of the geology of Torbay, it was declared a Geopark in 2007. As of 2022, the English Riviera UNESCO Global Geopark is one of 177 areas around the world to be endorsed by UNESCO, with the aim of using the geological heritage and linked environment, heritage and culture in these extraordinary places to help people understand and care for our remarkable shared planet. Geoparks also support sustainable economic development of the area, primarily through the development of geological tourism, including water-based activities like sea swimming.

FLORA AND FAUNA

Swimming in Torbay, you will see lots of wildlife. The waters here are particularly good for nature spotting, not just because of the variety of things to see, but because the geology itself has created a sheltered bay where the clarity and stillness of the water has great visibility. There are hundreds of varieties of seaweed, in a myriad of colours, as well as many different species of fish, crabs, corals, sponges and anemones. There are many sea birds, including cormorants, shags and oyster catchers, as well as guillemots and occasionally puffins. Large aquatic mammals like seals and dolphins are frequently seen.

Torbay's rich and diverse marine wildlife was recognised in 2009 as part of a wider Special Area of Conservation for its reefs and amazing seacaves, whilst in 2013, the Government designated it a Marine Conservation Zone, citing the 'high level of biodiversity in the area'. There are several different types of habitat in the Bay which support all manner of life. The soft sands are home to animals including heart urchins and brittle stars, while the rocky areas support sponges, sea squirts and seaweeds.

One of the most important and rarest habitats in the Bay is its seagrass beds. Seagrass is a flowering plant, the only one able to live in seawater and pollinate while submerged. It has long, bright green, ribbon-like leaves which are home to a wide range of animals including lobsters, seahorses and pipefish, as well as molluscs and worms. The beds also act as nursery areas to many species of fish. You can swim over sea grass beds in several places; they look like graceful green underwater meadows, and their presence is marked by special buoys to alert mariners so they don't anchor and cause damage.

SOCIAL SWIMMING

In recent years, what's become known as wild swimming has been enjoying a huge resurgence, fuelled by nostalgia, social networking, the proven health benefits and a thirst for some good old-fashioned fun and adventure. There are scores of Facebook groups, enabling people to meet up for everything from short dips to longer, endurance swims.

The health benefits of sea swimming include a boosted immune system, better circulation, hydrated skin, relaxed muscles and stress relief. Throw in weight loss (you'll burn more calories the colder the water), an increased libido and a wonderful natural high, and, quite frankly, everyone should be doing it!

There's also a growing awareness of the benefit of wild swimming for our mental health. A national group called Mental Health Swims (www.mentalhealthswims. co.uk) organises free meet ups, including one in Torbay. An organisation called HealthScape (www.healthscapecic.co.uk) also arranges regular swims around the Bay, aimed at boosting people's mental and physical health.

Another change is that swimming is now an all-year round activity. Turn up on a dull winter's day at high tide on any one of Torbay's beaches, and you are likely to find lots of people having a dip. Ten years ago, when we first wrote this book, that would never have happened. It's great that so many people are discovering what a joy outdoor swimming is, and how good it makes you feel.

The sea is free to use, making wild swimming just about the most inclusive activity there is. You need little or no equipment and indeed little of or no clothing - especially if you dare to bare at Petitor, Torbay's only nudist beach. Sea swimming is also really good for those with injuries or with limited mobility, while the open water has a complete disregard for age. We frequently bump into octogenarians and nonagenarians taking to the water with sprightly gusto.

Add in dawn swims, moonlight swims, solstice swims, Christmas swims, fancy dress swims and there really is something for everyone. There's even a group called 365 Swim Challenge (www.365seaswimchallenge. com), where people swim every day of the year, whilst raising funds for conservation and sea therapy.

Soon after writing the first edition of this book, we devised the Agatha Christie Sea Swim, a one-mile social swim that raises money for local charities. The swim was created as a celebration of the author's early life in the Bay and her love of sea swimming. The swim still takes place every year as part of the Agatha Christie Festival each September (www.agathachristiefestival.com). We alternate the routes of what we call a 'sightseeing swim' between beaches enjoyed by the author, including Beacon Cove to Meadfoot Beach and Broadsands Beach to Goodrington. Do join us one year if you can.

We hope this book inspires even more people to rediscover the joys of sea swimming and to hunt out some of the incredible wild swims of Torbay. The swims we will share take in geology, marine biology, history, and popular culture. We want to take you on some aquatic journeys; to discover the fascinating past that has brought us to where we are today, and to see the coastline from a fresh perspective.

This is our love letter to 22 very special miles of coastline and we do hope you enjoy it.

See you in the water!

PRACTICAL INFORMATION AND SAFETY

THE SWIMS

We have ordered the swims from north to south. None of the swims in this book involve swimming out to sea for any distance. They mostly hug the coastline, and you are never far from a 'getting out' spot.

The distances given are the total length, there and back. (all the swims are 'out and back'; on some you can walk back, or else walk to the start and swim back). We have tried to give accurate distances, but the lengths of the swims will vary according to the height of the tide. Also, the features described in the swims may or may not be visible, depending on whether the tide is high or low. For each swim we have tried to advise on the best state of the tide at which to swim it, in order to see the sights mentioned in the book. By the same token, if you swim at a different state of the tide, you may well see new exciting things that we haven't yet discovered! That's the joy of the ever-changing tidal world.

Postcodes, grid references and what3words locations refer to the parking spots.

TIDES

As mentioned above, tides are hugely significant for a sea swimmer. Always make sure you know what the tide is doing when you set off. You can buy tide tables in a range of local shops, including newsagents, garages, convenience stores and bookshops. They give the whole year's predictions; you can also check online but the times given on websites are only for the next seven days. Free tide apps also only cover the next seven days; if you want the whole year you have to pay a fee of a few pounds. Also, be aware that in the summer the online tide tables given by the BBC are in Greenwich Mean Time, not British Summer Time, so you have to add an hour on.

It is important to understand the difference between Spring and Neap tides. On a Spring tide (which is nothing to do with the season of Spring) there is far more water moving around. So, the tide comes in much further, and goes out much further, than on a Neap, when the difference between high and low water is less. You can use this information to your advantage. For example, if you swim at low water on a Spring tide, you will be able to see marine life that is normally hidden, covered up by the water. Similarly, you can choose to swim at high water on a Spring, when you know that the water will be deeper than normal; you might use this information to go on a swim around some particularly interesting rocks or islands. Spring tides occur around the time of the full and new moons, and your tide table will tell you when they are.

SEA TEMPERATURES

We all know that the water is warmest in the summer, but not many people realise that it is still pretty warm in October and November and even December. Indeed, in these months the water tends to be warmer than in the early summer. CEFAS (the Centre for Environment, Fisheries and Aquaculture Science) collates sea temperature readings from all over the country on its website. Taking Weymouth as an example (unfortunately there is no information for Torbay), readings taken over the last thirty years show that on average, the first three months of the year are coldest, at around 7 or 8 degrees C. In April, May, and June it starts to get warmer. The peak of warmth is in July, August and September, when temperatures double those of the first months of the year, hitting around 16 or 17 degrees. It's still pretty warm as the year goes on – for example in October it's 15 degrees and in November it's around 12 degrees.

KEEPING WARM

All of our swims can be done all the year round. The more you swim, the more you acclimatise. Everyone has different levels of tolerance of the cold, and you need to learn how much you can take. In general, it's a good idea to get out before you start to feel really cold. You lose a lot of heat through your head, so wear a swimming hat (it also of course helps you to be seen). Wearing a wetsuit is always a good idea when it's cold, and there are brilliant wetsuits which are purpose made for swimming, rather than surfing. Wetsuit gloves and boots are also a great way to keep warm, if you don't yet want to wear a wetsuit, but need extra protection against the cold. In the colder months of the year, it's vital to take warm clothing, particularly a woolly hat and socks, to change into immediately afterwards.

SAFETY FIRST

Never swim alone, and always tell someone where you're going. Don't swim when you've been drinking alcohol. Never jump or dive in without checking the depth first. If you are out swimming and are unsure if there's a current, swim a short distance and then swim back to see if it feels any different. Wear a brightly coloured swim cap and use a tow float to help you be seen, especially if you are in an area with a lot of boats, which is the case in certain parts of Torbay.

SEALS

Grey seals are often seen in Torbay, particularly on the quieter beaches of Maidencombe, Watcombe, Petitor, Churston, Fishcombe, Breakwater and St Mary's Bay. Common seals are also seen, but far less frequently. They are curious creatures, rather like dogs, and might well approach you. If this happens it is best to swim away from them calmly and quietly, avoiding sudden movements. They are unlikely to hurt you, but sometimes they like to explore with their mouths which can result in a bite. If this happens, seek medical advice as you may well need antibiotics. If swimming in an area where you know there are seals, and you are concerned, wear a wetsuit and gloves and boots so your body is protected.

The general rule is to stay away from seals as they are wild animals and human interaction is stressful for them. Any disturbance to seals threatens their survival. This applies both in the water and on land. If you see a seal hauled out on a rock or the beach, do not approach it. Seals use enormous amounts of energy hunting, and need this time to rest.

Pupping season occurs between September and December. Be particularly careful to avoid seals at this time. If you see a pup on a beach, stay away from it. Its parents will be nearby, even if you can't see them.

THE SEA SWIMMERS' CODE

- Do not leave litter, and pick up any rubbish that you find, particularly plastic. Support the #2minutebeachclean campaign.

- Respect other water users, such as anglers and kayakers.

- Give seals space. Do not approach them and swim away if they approach you.

- Do nothing to damage the ecosystem.

- Know your tides.

- Leave only footprints, take only memories.

WILD SWIMMING TOP TIPS

Useful tips from our fellow Devon wild swimmers

• Choose your swimming friends carefully. My favourite are those who can bake cakes. *Faye Webb*

• I have a recipe for lemon drizzle cake which incorporates ginger, chilli powder and gin to warm the outdoor swimmer! *Jonathan Joyce*

• Take a tea towel to stand on after a swim. On cold days it keeps your feet warm on concrete. *Jackie Wills*

• Always carry a swimsuit and a towel in your car; you never know when there will be an opportunity to jump in the water. I also swear by hot Ribena! *Jane Brown*

• I take along my 'portable shower in a bucket'. Fill two old hot water bottles with hot (not boiling) water and a little body wash at home. Wrap in a towel and take to your swim in one of those plastic trugs with handles. After the swim, stand in the trug and pour the warm soapy water over yourself. My patented portable shower system! Works every time! *Stephanie Simon*

• I swear by a plastic-backed picnic rug, perfect for standing on when getting changed on a damp beach. *Ellie Ricketts*

• I take a paintbrush with me to the beach so I can brush the sand off my feet – saves getting sand in the socks. *Christine Newbury (Matt's Mum!)*

• Make sure your significant other has been briefed on exactly how to dry you properly, dress you to an appropriate standard and feed you sips of hot rum chocolate when your hands are so cold they won't work! *Clare Pettinger*

• Ladies – when getting changed after swimming in the winter, don't even bother to try and put your bra back on. *Anna Dunscombe*

• Be aware that cold hands increase your risk of dropping your towel when changing. I underestimated this risk and mooned a group of geology students at Oddicombe! *Matthew Jeanes*

• Instead of ear plugs I use blue tack (or white tack is better as it's softer – a tip from a lovely blonde surfer chap. *Rosie Barnfield*

• Make sure you vaseline up for long sea swims to avoid chafing – but always get someone else to apply it to avoid foggy goggles! *Sadie Crapper*

• Turn your socks the right way out before your swim, as your hands will not work after. *Jonathan Joyce*

• A fleecy onesie is very handy to put on after a winter swim to give a warm layer before putting the rest of your clothes on. *Jill Hutchinson*

• Keep your knickers in the pocket of your trousers so you can find them after the swim. *Lynne Roper*

• Dance after swimming! *Lesley Chapman*

MAIDENCOMBE TO BELL ROCK

An enchanting swim along the coast to
one of the Bay's two natural arches.

Maidencombe feels like the archetypal chocolate-box Devon village. Steep and winding narrow lanes lead down to where the hamlet nestles in a hideaway combe. At its heart is an ancient manor house, the Courthouse, with a Judas tree thought to have been brought back from the Lebanon in the 16th century; there is a thatched gastro pub, and Maidencombe Farm sits in the centre of it all, with plants and flowers always for sale on its front stone steps.

It's a short stroll down the hill from the pub to the beach. A stream tumbles down alongside the steps down to the shore and we are convinced the cove is the inspiration for the setting of a novella by Mary Shelley (author of Frankenstein). *Maurice or the Fisher's Cot* was written in 1820, after Mary had a holiday in Torquay with her husband, Percy Bysshe Shelley. It is set in Torquay and tells of a boy who has lost his parents and a father whose son has been abducted.

The boy grows up with an old fisherman, and the description of the beach and the cottage sounds very like Maidencombe. "Old Barnet's cottage is situated about three miles from this town at the foot of the cliff…the spring tide comes up almost to the steps of the door…it is sheltered by the crag. Beside it is a little cove where the fishing boat is kept…a number of pretty flowers grow beside the brook which comes running down from the tall, red cliff."

When you get down to the cove you will see huge red blocks of sandstone everywhere, as though a baby giant has thrown his toy bricks out of his pram. They litter the bottom of the cliffs. The views out to sea are stunning; you can see over to the Jurassic Coast of East Devon and Dorset, and in the other direction you can see the Ore Stone, off Hope's Nose, lurking on the horizon.

The swim route heads directly south, hugging the coastline, along to Bell Rock, a diminutive rock arch which is a little further down the coast towards Torquay. It's best to swim around low tide, which gives you more space to swim through the arch under the Bell. Set off from the right hand side of the beach, and swim out of the cove to the right. The water is a wonderful shade of dark green here; perhaps because of the redness of the cliffs. If you keep close in to the shore you will swim over underwater gardens of kelp and other seaweeds, and there's a good chance of seeing fish and other marine life. One summer's day we once saw starfish, wrasse, prawns and a huge spider crab which glowed neon orange underwater.

You can admire the red cliffs as you swim along. There is a softness about them; perhaps because of the patches of green fields on the tops, and the woods and vegetation which cover large areas of the sandstone. Some people, though, find the red cliffs oppressive. The author Rudyard Kipling stayed in Rock House, which overlooks the sea here, in 1896. He described it as "stuck on the side of a steep hill falling away…to a hundred-foot cliff of pure red soil." And yet despite the apparent idyll, he and his wife became sunk in a depression which wouldn't shift. In the end they left early, convinced there was something about the house itself which was affecting their mood.

You will soon see a vast slab of rock, Shackley Bench, sticking out at right angles from the bottom of the cliff and sloping starkly into the sea. Seabirds like to gather here in large flocks, and just beyond it is an area that some local people call the Lagoon. The upright side of the Bench forms the northern border of the pool, with its sheer walls dropping down into the water. It's a fun place to frolic, jumping off the Bench when the tide is high enough. (Always check the depth before doing this).

Don't be surprised if you see a seal pop up. This happened to us once. It kept its distance but stayed with us for some time. If it makes you nervous you can sit on Shackley Bench or one of the various other rocky outcrops for a while. The best advice is to stay calm and avoid eye contact. Swim slowly as fast movement can spook them.

Your destination of Bell Rock should now be well in sight. It really does look like a bell. It's a lovely cone shape, topped with a grass crew-cut. As you approach, it's not immediately apparent that you can swim through; it looks as though there's just a small hole in the rock through which you can see a tiny patch of sky. But the nearer you get, you start to see a slit through the middle of the rock, and you see the light shining through from the other side. Depending on the angle, and also the height of the tide, the space looks like an hour glass, or the eye of a needle.

Swimming through the archway can be a very varied experience, depending on the tide and the movement of the sea. On a calm day you can pootle through, marvelling at the angles of the rock, the light and shade, and

the luxuriant fronds of thick, shiny kelp lining your passageway. When the sea's a bit rougher though, it can be a bit of a rollercoaster, as you're swept through, moving vertically up and down with the sea's motion, surrounded by swinging seaweed, pulled this way and that. Watch your head!

When you get through, turn around and admire the mass of the Bell looming behind you. You can either swim back through, or swim around it, before starting the journey back to the beach. As you approach the cove, its remoteness is a reminder of its smuggling past; it was the ideal place to bring in contraband, which was apparently often stored in the farmhouses in the village, before being taken on to its final destination.

If you've got the energy, the rocks on the northern side of the beach have some wonderful platforms, ledges and drops, perfect for diving and snorkelling. And if it's the summer time, you can get refreshments at the café. How nice to sit and and have a well-earned hot chocolate, overlooking the scene of your latest aquatic exploration.

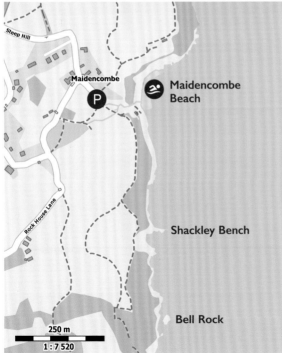

INFORMATION

SWIM ROUTE: Swim out of the cove and turn right, heading south with the shore on your right. Swim past Shackley Bench and then down to Bell Rock, then return the same way.

DISTANCE: 0.8 miles.

BEST TIDE STATE: Mid to low tide.

SWIM HIGHLIGHT: Swim through the rock arch at Bell Rock.

GET OUT POINTS: Shackley Bench; rocks by Bell Rock.

POTENTIAL HAZARDS: There are quite a few seals in the area. Be especially careful during pupping season in the Autumn. If you are tempted to dive off Shackley Bench, check the depth first.

DOGS: Allowed all year round.

PARKING: Car park above the beach: TQ1 4XS, SX 926 684, What3Words: fatigued.zapped.greeting.

PUBLIC TRANSPORT: The 22 bus between Dawlish and South Devon College calls at Maidencombe Cross on the main coast road: from there it is a walk of about 1/3 of a mile down to the beach.

REFRESHMENTS: Café Rio on the beach is open April to October and sells sandwiches, burgers and other light bites. 01803 317737. The Thatched Tavern, just up from the beach has pub classics including fish and chips and steaks as well as lighter options including salads. 01803 327140.

EASIER ACCESS: Although the car park is close to the beach, there is a set of steep steps down.

WATCOMBE, WHITE BEACH AND THE JADE CAVE

A stunning swim from one of Torquay's more isolated beaches, taking in a swim-through tunnel and smugglers' caves.

I t's worth taking a pause when you arrive at the car park above Watcombe Beach, not only because it is just about the only free car park in Torquay, but to get a glimpse of what was once one of the biggest tourist attractions in the Bay. Valley of the Rocks is the dramatic name once given to the area dominated by a dome-shaped sandstone outcrop known as Giant Rock. Lush woodland now masks the 50-metre-high landmark, especially in the summer months, but it is still just about discernible if you stand in the corner of the car park where a footpath heads north into the woods.

Back in Victorian times this was an open area of common land owned in part by Isambard Kingdom Brunel. The towering rocks made it a stunning setting for social gatherings including an amazing Grand Gala and Fête Champetre back in 1853. Organised by the Torquay Choral Society, the celebration festival featured a 1000-strong choir enjoyed by more than 7000 spectators. Giant Rock was illuminated, and the climax saw a military tattoo in which a Highland Regiment beat a retreat from the summit.

To find the beach, you need to leave the car park where you drove in, and turn left down the road which soon becomes a track. There is an official sign on the gate telling you the beach is closed, but it is still perfectly possible to visit and to swim from. Part of the steps have fallen away, but there is an alternative path and it is no more inaccessible than many other places along the coast.

Walking down, the towering trees create a feeling of the ancient and legendary, a place where Jurassic beasts may still roam and magic is possible. There is definitely a sense of the jungle about the approach down to the shore. As you head down the steep path you'll cross the South West Coastal Path before noticing how the vegetation dips significantly into an undulating valley to your left. This is the site of former clay pits which provided the raw material used at The Watcombe Pottery, which existed for almost a century.

It's always a really special moment when you first spot the sea through the trees and one of the Bay's most beautiful beaches comes into view. The history of the beach as a tourist spot owes everything to two men called Herbert Goulding and Samuel Honeywill.

After returning from the horrors of the First World War, the two old school friends decided to hack a pathway down to the beach where they built a refreshment hut in 1923, carrying materials from Oddicombe Beach by boat.

Living in a tent behind the hut, they rented out rowing boats and sold refreshments, with water and milk being carried down the hill in churns, along with the other provisions. By the 1930s they had built a larger hut complete with a veranda, as well as more huts for their families to sleep in during the summer season. As the business prospered, they also introduced ferries, which would carry people around to Teignmouth, Babbacombe and beyond.

Sadly, their business came to end during the Second World War, when tank traps were laid on the beach. Mr Goulding died before the end of the conflict, while Mr Honeywill's eldest son was killed at Mandalay.

After the war, the café was revived, and, during the 1950s and 1960's became hugely popular again, with all of the customers served by staff carrying Watcombe Pottery on trays. At the time of writing the café is in a state of disrepair due to storm damage and vandalism, but there are plans by Torbay Council to make significant repairs to the beach and its access, so we can only hope.

The steep walk down to the beach means it tends to be one of the quietest in Torbay, but that's not to say it doesn't get busy. The waters

are very popular with scuba divers, while scouts from the nearby camp come down to the beach for adventure games and training exercises. The beach is also popular with wild swimmers, including those training to cross the Channel.

The beach itself is east facing and sheltered by Watcombe Head, making it safe for swimming. Mainly comprised of shingle and red sand, there are some larger rocks in the water, so it's well worth wearing some form of swim footwear, which will also allow you to scramble onto the many rocks along the route. There are also some amazing breccia boulders on the beach, which along with red sandstone will become a very familiar sight

along our route.

This swim takes you from the left of the beach as you face the sea, around the headland, past a secret beach and on to some amazing swim-through caves, before returning south past Watcombe to visit a fascinating smugglers cave.

Swimming towards the jumble of fallen rocks to your left you'll soon actually be swimming over the entrance to Watcombe Caves, an underwater passageway only accessible by scuba divers, fish and the local friendly seal. It's believed the passages lead almost up to Kent's Cavern and local divers report being able to enter a huge underwater domed cavern in an air pocket, complete with impressive stalactites.

As you round the corner of the headland, you'll be able to see what's known locally as White Beach (although it is called Whitsand Beach on the Ordnance Survey map). This is one of several secret coves accessible to wild swimmers around the Bay. It's easy to imagine this beach resembling Watcombe before the path was built and the cafe introduced. A blanket of green vegetation covers the red cliffs, and with a little imagination it's possible to spot pillars within the foliage, including one that resembles Rapunzel's tower, complete with spiral staircase and windows looking out to freedom. Don't bother rescuing her, she's not very nice.

Swimming onwards with the beach on your left, you'll approach another striking

red sandstone cliff, topped with green. The erosion has created what resembles dental decay and cavities in the rock face, with the stain of minerals washing down the cliffs like carelessly gargled mouthwash. Further on it's possible to see what appear to be gargoyles in the cliffs, or sinister wax faces melted in the heat. It doesn't seem to put off the gulls, who perch in the nooks and crannies.

Swimming onwards, the base of the cliffs is coated in seaweed, like spinach stewed beyond the point of edibility by a vindictive school dinner lady. The erosion of the breccia above is particularly noticeable, with large stones waiting to fall down to their new home beneath the waves. You'll soon spot what we've called the Kraken's Cave, which is definitely worth exploring if you dare. Water flowing into unseen parts of the cave creates a deep rumbling sound, like the tummy of a hungry sea monster.

Emerging out from the cave and looking towards your left, you'll be able to see the entrance to a swim-through which leads to what we've named The Jade Cave. The passage through the rock caves is actually the shape of an hour glass laid on its side, and as you enter through the top, you'll be able to see tiny black mussels clustered together on the walls, like jet-coloured jewels. On one especially memorable occasion the walls of the cave were completely covered in starfish. Half way along you'll see light from another channel off to your right, while as you continue to gently float through the cavern, Bell Rock will soon become visible through the far end of the tunnel.

Swim back around the outside of the cave and back in through the side entrance and towards your original entry point. If you are lucky enough to catch the light just at the right time, an amazing optical effect happens. The water appears to be lit from underneath, giving the water a psychedelic green/yellow iridescence – hence the name The Jade Cave. It's an amazingly tranquil experience and a secret you'll be eager to share with someone special.

Swimming back towards your start point,

it's worth taking a pause and bobbing around in a circle to take in the panorama. On a clear day you'll be able to see The Ore Stone straight ahead, as well as the teeth of Long Quarry Point and the inviting sight of the Cary Arms. Look back in the other direction and you'll see The Ness sheltering Teignmouth and then Dawlish, Starcross, Exmouth and perhaps even as far as Dorset.

Obviously, you can just swim back to the start if you are feeling tired, but if you want to

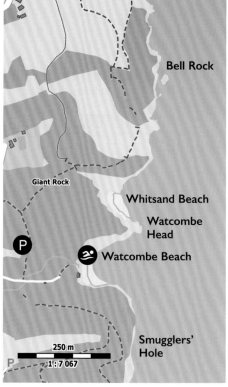

extend the adventure, swim on south past the beach at Watcombe, and immediately on the right you will find a sequence of caves called Smugglers' Hole. The cliffs in this direction seem more imposing and dramatic and it's easy to let your imagination drift back to a time of smugglers and pirates.

As you approach the caves, you'll notice avian sentries on duty in natural sentry boxes carved by nature within what we have dubbed Cormorant Cliff. The iridescence of the birds' plumage seems really enhanced by the red of the cliffs in the background as they stand like statues in niches guarding the caves.

Smuggler's Hole was once huge - big enough to get a longboat in. Legend has it that hundreds of years ago a tunnel once extended all the way back to the church in St Mary-church, where the parson would receive the contraband and distribute it to his wayward flock. Sadly, rock falls mean the tunnel is now blocked, but you can still swim into the caves. The more daring may even like to swim through the first triangular entrance through a very fishy smelling cavern and through a tight channel into the second cave and around into a third.

The swim back to the beach is always beautiful, the red of the tranquil cove perfectly topped by a palette of green. It's a steep but rewarding walk back up through the woods to the car park and you'll certainly have warmed up by the time you reach the top. But the steep hill is what keeps Watcombe Beach a nice quiet treat, loved by the locals and us wild swimmer alike.

INFORMATION

SWIM ROUTE: Swim along the left-hand side of the cove and turn left, swimming north with the shore on your left. You pass White Beach and after that you will find the Kraken's Cave and the Jade Cave on your left. You can carry on to Bell Rock, or else turn around and swim back to the cove at Watcombe. Here you can extend the swim south of the cove, to find the Smugglers' Hole caves before turning back to the beach.

DISTANCE: 0.8 miles.

BEST TIDE STATE: Mid to low tide.

SWIM HIGHLIGHT: Exploring the Jade Cave and Kraken's Cave as well as the 'secret' White Beach.

GET OUT POINTS: White Beach.

POTENTIAL HAZARDS: Caves can be dangerous during rough water or a swell; do not enter in these conditions. Care should be taken on the steep walk down, especially around broken steps. Seals are also often seen here. If one approaches, swim quietly away, avoiding sudden movements.

DOGS: Dogs allowed all year round.

PARKING: Watcombe Beach Car Park (space for 30 vehicles). Steep walk to beach. TQ1 4SH SX 922 673, What3Words drop.deeply.curl

PUBLIC TRANSPORT: The 22 bus between Dawlish and South Devon College (Paignton) will take you to Teignmouth Road. Get off the bus near Watcombe Beach Road. 1/3 mile walk down to beach.

REFRESHMENTS: None at the beach, but for a treat, The Orestone Manor, TQ1 4SX 01803 897511 serves afternoon tea between 2pm and 4pm. It was where the first Christmas card was designed.

EASIER ACCESS: Unfortunately the beach is a 10-minute walk down a fairly steep and rough path.

Swim 3

ODDICOMBE
AND THE JULIET CAVE

An adventurous swim to a double-chambered
cave and past the site of a historic quarry

As you stand on the top of Babbacombe Downs, looking at the
vast spread of the ocean before
you, you are on one of the highest cliff top
promenades in Britain. You are three hundred
feet above sea level, and on a clear day you can
see all the way over to Portland Bill in Dorset.
It's a steep climb down to Oddicombe Beach
below; you have two options: walking down
the hairpin bend road or getting the eccentric
Cliff Railway which trundles up and down.

Before you do either, stop to look at the
statue of the woman at the top of the road
down to the beach. She stands, with a bird
perched on her hand, usually holding fresh
flowers, put there by we know not who.
She's Georgina, Baroness Mount-Temple, a
Victorian anti-vivisection campaigner. She
lived at nearby Babbacombe Cliff, where she
fed the birds from her veranda.

Lady Mount-Temple was well-connected.
She knew John Ruskin and the pre-Raphaelite
painters, and her cousin was Constance, the
wife of Oscar Wilde. One summer Oscar
came to stay – without his wife – and it was
here that he started his affair with Alfred,
Lord Douglas and from where he wrote the
romantic letters used in the trial against him.
He spent four months living it up in Torquay,
and according to his biographer, Rupert
Croft-Cooke, "There was no time happier,
more irresponsibly mirthful and untroubled
by cares of any kind".

The Babbacombe Cliff Railway was built by
the Torquay Tramways Company and opened
in 1926, and it's a fun way to travel down to
the beach. You can even get married in it if
you want. They stop the car half way down
to enable the ceremony to take place. Enjoy
the framed view of pure blue sea in front of
you as you descend. Queen Victoria came
here in 1845 and described it in her journal
as being like Italy, with wooded hills. She
said it reminded her of a ballet or play where
"'nymphs appear, such rocks and grottos, with
deepest sea on which there was no ripple".

When you arrive down at the beach you are
struck by how pretty it is, and can see why
it started to become a place of recreation in
the early nineteenth century. One tourist
guide of the 1820s describes it as a 'romantic
rocky glen', and rich families started to build
summer houses there. It is sheltered, with vast
open views, with wooded cliffs above.

The cliffs though, tell their own and somewhat disturbing story. Just past the café you can see tumbledown piles of great lumps of red sandstone, from a huge cliff fall in 2010; the cliff has a raw red scar where the land fell away, smashing the promenade below. Shortly after this fall, there was another one, and a house at the top of the cliffs collapsed and was completely lost. There have been other, minor falls since and so the northern part of the beach is now officially out of bounds.

You can hire a beach hut for the day, or else get changed on the beach. The swim is best done at low tide. Start your swim in the middle of the cove, opposite the café, and head north. The red cliffs to your left are sandstone from the Permian period, 300-250 million years ago, when Torbay was like the Sahara; it was incredibly dry and hot. The distinctive red comes from the iron in the rock which oxidised in the sweltering heat. Geologist Professor Ian West says this is one of the 'few places in Southern

England where you can walk on the surface of a harsh desert.' Swim along past the cliff fall and approach the two red sandstone stacks towards the end of the beach.

At the end of the beach, you'll discover a concrete platform built into the rocks, with a staircase leading down towards the water. This is the Gentlemen's Bathing Place – and you can just see the remains of the old ceramic tiles which identified it as such – just like the name of a street on a wall. This was where the men swam in the days of segregated swimming; and it was here, in 1922, that the Oddicombe Swimming Club was formed, by a group of men who regularly bathed there together. The club is still going strong today, and has an annual swim off the beach every summer.

Swim along the coast from the Gents' Bathing Place, keeping the shore on your left. You are now going past Devonian limestone – this is even older than the sandstone next to it, and dates back around 400 million years. At this point Torbay was near the equator, and was a lush, tropical, and warm sea inhabited by all manner of marine life. The limestone is actually made of millions of corals which melded together to form the rock, and as you swim out towards the northern, outer corner of the beach, you can see the outlines of some of the corals, encrusted with barnacles.

As you turn the corner of the headland, look out for an opening in the rock. If it's low tide, it leads to the most unusual double-chambered cavern, that we've called the Juliet Cave. As you swim towards the cave, look out for

white and pink Dead Man's fingers on the rocks along the entrance. These are fleshy corals that look a bit like dripping candlewax (or a dead man's fingers if you are of a more gruesome bent). Under the water they open out, rather like anemones. Local diver Dan Bolt, an award-winning underwater photographer, says the pink ones are particularly rare, so do not touch them; admire only. Our friend Lynne, who is sadly no longer with us, once described the shocking pink of these corals as 'the colour of Katie Price's jodhpurs'. Swim into the cave, but be careful if it is at all choppy; if there is any swell you could get swept in and hurt.

The cave snakes in to the right of the opening, and to the left you can climb up a smooth pink rocky slope. At the top you will find a narrow opening to another cave which is, as it were, 'upstairs'. You cross it in the gloom, wading through a pebbly pool, and on the other side there is a 'window' or balcony looking down on the cave below. Hence why we dubbed it the Juliet Cave. Such inner architecture is quite extraordinary, and as your eyes get used to the gloom, enjoy the feeling of being enclosed in a secret space.

Leave the cave the way you came in, and you are then greeted to the sight of a vast expanse of turquoise water, through which you originally swam. From here, it looks – and indeed is – like the perfect swimming pool.

Come out of the cave and continue to swim north with the shore on your left. Above you are the remains of an old quarry, where they used to dig out limestone which was used to build many of the houses locally. Our friend Jackie's dad, Jim Wills, who lived in Torquay all his life, once showed us a drawing, dating from the 1840s, picturing an unusual hexagonal foreman's hut on the edge of the site, by the sea; there was also a thatched fisherman's cottage there. Although the foreman's hut is long gone, Jim found a hexagonal shaped pillar on the beach, which was no doubt part of that building. He was an incredible fount of knowledge on everything to do with local history, and was very helpful to us when we were researching this book; he died in 2020 and is much missed.

Keep going; you are now swimming over

a kelp forest. Look out for groups of starfish clinging to the rocks and sea bed below. A short way along is Petit Tor Cove, a well-known naturist beach. The local etiquette is apparently single men on the left, women, couples and families on the right (looking out to sea, so it's the opposite if you're approaching from the sea).

At this point, it's time to turn and head back. As you do, admire the pinnacles of Long

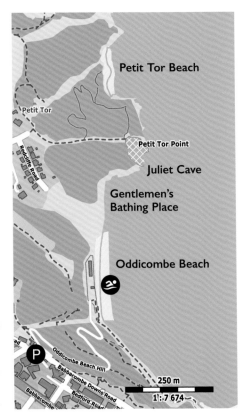

Quarry Point which you will see ahead of you, at the southern end of the Bay. This is another abandoned quarry, with quite a fairy tale air.

Do you remember we mentioned the Devonian period 400 million years ago, when Devonian limestone was formed? Well, it was a period of huge tectonic movement, with land masses sliding around the earth, and massive earthquakes. These have left fault lines; a particularly notable one is right in front of you as you leave the water. Where? Well, if you look at the cliff railway, that's where it is. The engineers, back in the 1920s, took advantage of the natural cleft in the rock, to construct their railway line. A thought to carry with you as you travel in the railway car back up to the Downs.

INFORMATION

SWIM ROUTE: From the middle of the beach, swim out and then turn left, heading north with the shore on your left. Pass the headland at the northern end of the beach and turn left to find the Juliet Cave. After a visit to the cave, carry on swimming north past the old quarry until you reach Petitor (naturist) beach. At this point turn round and swim back the way you came.

DISTANCE: 0.6 miles.

BEST TIDE STATE: Mid to low tide.

SWIM HIGHLIGHT:
The Juliet Cave.

GET OUT POINTS: There are rocks you can rest on just by the site of the old quarry.

POTENTIAL HAZARDS: Falling rocks from the cliffs at the northern end of the beach. You should be fine swimming as you are some distance from the cliffs, but it's not advisable to walk under them. Caves can be dangerous during rough water or a swell; do not enter in these conditions.

DOGS: Not allowed between 1 May and 30 September.

PARKING: Free on Babbacombe Downs Road: TQ1 3LN, SX 924 656, What3Words: metals.spring.poetic.

PUBLIC TRANSPORT: The 22 bus between Dawlish and South Devon College stops on Babbacombe

Road a short walk from the beach.

REFRESHMENTS: The Cliff Railway Café, above the beach has stunning views out to sea and serves lovely cakes as well as jacket potatoes, soup and sandwiches. 01803 324025 Three Degrees Café is on the beach and is open Wednesday to Sunday, serving tapas as well as well as sandwiches and burgers. 01803 311202. For a treat, you can walk over to the Cary Arms on nearby Babbacome Beach (01803 327110).

EASIER ACCESS: From the cliff railway it is only a few steps to the beach. There is a slipway you can use to enter the water.

ANSTEY'S COVE TO REDGATE BEACH AND THE HIDDEN POOL

An exciting swim to an abandoned beach, and then to a pool hidden behind the mysterious pinnacle of Long Quarry Point

A swim from Anstey's Cove over to the officially closed Redgate Beach has a slightly naughty air to it – the kind of old school adventure that we wild swimmers thrive on. In order to access the pool, you will need to do this swim on high water, when the cove also looks its sparkling best. The adventure starts with the walk down to the beach which is absolutely magical. At the top of the hill, you look down on a scene that looks like a fairy tale. The pointed pinnacle of Long Quarry Point, at the far side of the cove, frames it beautifully, and lends an air of mystery. The path down is fringed by woods.

Ansteys Cove is a beautiful shingle beach and from the 1890s to the 1930s people arriving at the stunning spot would have been greeted with the following sign:

Picnics supplied with hot water and tea
At a nice little house down by the sea
Fresh crabs and lobsters every day
Salmon peel sometimes red mullet and grey
The neatest of pleasure boats let out on hire
Fishing tackle as good as you can desire
Bathing machines for ladies are kept

With towels and gowns, all quite correct
THOMAS is the man who provides everything
And also teaches young people to swim

The Thomas family had a refreshment hut and bathing machines until 1929 when the council bought the beach concessions from Jonathan Thomas for £7000. Interestingly, the nearby prehistoric caves at Kents Cavern have been owned and operated by the Powe family for five generations and were bought by Francis Powe in 1903. He was a carpenter and used the caves to make beach furniture, beach huts and boats for both Ansteys Cove and Meadfoot Sands. A visit to the caves is fascinating and should be on any holiday itinerary.

Walk down towards the sea and look to your left. Nowhere is the complex relationship between man and nature more apparent than here. Ahead you'll be able to see a huge limestone headland called Walls Hill, dating back around 370-390 million years to the Devonian period. It was an important time in terms of evolution as it was during this period that animals were just beginning to venture onto the land. And perhaps it's something in our genetic make-up hundreds of millions of years later that draws wild swimmers back to that sea.

At the summit of the cliffs is a large flat limestone plateau that was once an Iron Age fortification, where tribal groups gathered during times of threat. Today it's popular with walkers and offers spectacular views across the Bay. To the right you'll see a curious pointed rock formation like a steeple, or the tooth of some Jurassic monster in desperate need of a dentist. This is Long Quarry Point and limestone was mined from here to be used in the mansions and civic buildings of Torquay during Victorian times.

Of course, man can never tame nature, and coastal erosion and rock falls have now sadly led to the closure of Redgate Beach, which is around to the left of the promenade. In the past it was also known as White Beach, presumably because of the brilliance of its shingle. If the writers of this book could be Mayor for a day, our first task would be to make the cliffs safe again in order to reopen this really special and much-loved little beach.

The area does remain well used though, especially by rock climbers. Anstey's Cove has some of the best and toughest sport climbing in Britain. It's also a popular spot for coasteering, an adventure activity that combines cliff jumping, swimming and rock climbing.

The swim starts from the tiny rocky beach below the café. This area was popular with

rich Victorians, whose servants had the unenviable task of lugging down huge baskets of picnic food to enjoy, as hardworking fisherman mended their nets nearby. Indeed the "Queen of Crime" (and thanks to her passion for wild swimming – "Queen of the Brine") Agatha Christie recalls a romantic moonlit picnic here in her autobiography.

It was with a gentleman called Amyas Boston, a fellow cast member in a play that the young Agatha was performing in at Cockington Court. They sat on this very beach holding hands and not speaking. As a somewhat backhanded tribute she later borrowed his first name for a murder victim in her novel *Five Little Pigs*.

Enter the water carefully, there are lots of submerged rocks here and footwear is recommended. The cafe owners sometimes try to clear a path down the beach and into the water by moving hundreds of the smaller rocks, but it's a Canute of a task and the tide and nature soon restore order. However, the water here is usually incredibly clear, with this spot winning annual "Quality Coast Awards," so wear goggles or a mask and a snorkel to enjoy the wonderful palette of this underwater world.

Swim out of the little cove alongside the promenade on your left. Keep an eye out for difficult-to-spot fishing lines cast by anglers sitting on the rocks – you don't want to end up as the catch of the day. Soon the stones and pebbles below the surface, that are remnants of a nearby quarry, give way to sand and the challenge is to hold your breath, swim down and grab a handful. It's also worth keeping

an eye out for man-made objects buried in the sand. One of the meanings of Ansteys is "narrow cove" and this area has provided the perfect spot for illegal imports throughout the centuries.

Back in the 19th century smugglers would make regular trips across to the Channel Islands and the continent to load up their boats with valuable cargoes of tobacco and spirits. The sheltered cove and woods around Ansteys Cove made it the perfect place to hide the contraband for later collection.

In more recent times, in October 1988, the area gained the nickname Cannabis Cove after police and customs officials caught

modern-day smugglers unloading £5m worth of the drug from a trawler, called The Etoile de Lisieux, into a small inflatable dinghy. By the time of the trial, some 70 bales had been recovered, some trawled from the bottom of the sea, where it had been thrown overboard. At the time there were lots of rumours about fishermen inadvertently hooking bales of the drug. If nothing else the fish must have been easier to catch, especially the lethargic and apathetic ones, displaying curious cases of the munchies.

At the end of the promenade, turn left, following the coastline around the small headland which is called Devil's Point. If you look up at the cliffs here you will be able to see old bits of concrete which once supported an elegant wooden walkway, that led around from the promenade at Anstey's over to Redgate Beach. It was in regular use throughout most of the twentieth century, enabling people to enjoy this gorgeous location. Old film from the 60s shows how the beach was absolutely packed in the summer. It's sad that this beautiful cove is no longer accessible to walkers, but as swimmers, it's not a problem. It's a great feeling reaching the shore on this sand and shingle beach, which is usually deserted unless anyone else has paddled in from an anchored yacht or attempted to scramble down the dangerous cliffs.

It's a wonderful suntrap and a great place to close your eyes and drift back in time, perhaps hearing the playful echoes of children's laugher, the gentle chug of the small ferry that once serviced the beach, the yelps

of families braving the cool waters and the excited chatter as people queued for ice creams at the busy little kiosk. In the past we have tried to recreate these halcyon days by hosting both a 1970's and 1980's themed swim party here.

After relaxing on the beach, you can set off for the next stage of the swim. Head out along the left hand (northern) side of Redgate Beach, towards the pointed fang protruding from Long Quarry Point. Just past the pinnacle, there is a narrow channel, where the combination of the rocks and the light makes the water a particularly intense turquoise. Swim into the channel, and at the end you will find

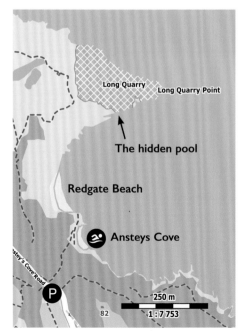

a gap above a large segment of rock. Climb over the rock and you will find a concealed cave with a perfect, hidden, swimming pool, complete with a natural skylight in the roof.

On a summer's day, when the sunbeams burst through, it is very special. However, please take note of an important safety consideration here: before jumping into the pool, you must make sure you can get out. We were once so excited we leapt in without thinking, only to realise that getting out involved dragging ourselves up a sheer wall of rock. The ideal height of tide you need is higher than 4.7 metres, both for climbing in and out.

To complete the swim, you can head straight back across the bay to where you started, or, if you prefer, return the way you came, taking in another stop at Redgate Beach.

This secluded gem is so beautiful, that on a sunny day many yachts drop anchor here, and it's hard to believe you are at the English seaside, not in some secluded millionaire's retreat in the Mediterranean. But you don't need a penny to enjoy this swim, just a swimming costume, some goggles, some fellow adventurers and a healthy appetite for exploring. And, regardless of what the signs say, wild swimmers have an Access All Areas pass.

INFORMATION

SWIM ROUTE: From the beach below the café, swim alongside the promenade on your left. At the end of the prom, turn left, continuing to hug the coastline until you arrive at Redgate Beach. After a rest at Redgate, swim out along the left hand (northern) side of the beach, until you reach the large, witch's hat shaped pinnacle at Long Quarry Point. Just past the pinnacle turn left up a narrow channel. At the end of the channel, climb over the rock to find the hidden pool. After, you can take the same route back, or else make it a circle by swimming directly across the bay back to Anstey's Cove.

DISTANCE: 0.6 miles.

BEST TIDE STATE: High tide. You need a tide of at least 4.7 metres to access the hidden pool.

SWIM HIGHLIGHT: The hidden pool.

GET OUT POINTS: Redgate Beach.

POTENTIAL HAZARDS: Anstey's Cove is very rocky so swim shoes are advisable. If entering the hidden pool, make sure you can get out before jumping in. Seals are also sometimes around here; if one approaches, swim away slowly and quietly, avoiding sudden movements.

DOGS: Allowed all year round.

PARKING: Anstey's Cove car park: TQ1 2JE, SX 934 645, What3Words: erase.yard.middle. You can also park on Ilsham Road and walk across Stoodley Meadow: TQ1 2JD, SX 935 642, What3Words: notion.parade.voted.

PUBLIC TRANSPORT: The 22 bus between Dawlish and South Devon College stops on Babbacombe Road a short walk from the beach. 32 Bus operates between Torquay Harbour and Wellswood.

REFRESHMENTS: Anstey's Cove Café is open in the summer months and does cooked breakfasts as well as nachos and burgers. 07780 554603. The Me and Mrs Jones Deli in nearby Ilsham Road serves tasty salads and pies. 01803 298745.

EASIER ACCESS: From the car park, it's a 5-minute walk downhill along either a tarmac path or steps to the beach. There are then steps down to the water, but the beach is uneven and rocky so shoes are advised.

Swim 5

MEADFOOT
AND ITS ISLANDS

An exciting circular route around the bay off
Meadfoot beach, visiting West Shag and East Shag Rocks

There is a sense of grandeur about Meadfoot. The coastline sweeps in an elegant curve, echoed in the beautiful crescent of the Osborne Hotel, which overlooks the beach. This was built in the mid nineteenth century, and was described at the time as 'the finest crescent of houses in Western England.' Not only that, Charles Darwin stayed here in 1861, where he completed his ground-breaking work, *The Origin of Species.*

Whether or not the huge 1960s tower block, Kilmorie Flats, which also dominates the bay, adds or detracts from its appeal, is a matter of opinion. It's posh apartments, but it's still a tower block. Whatever, this is a spectacular swim, taking in huge views of Torbay, great chunks of cliff and various islands. In fact, it's great if you've never swum to an island before, because you can do so on this swim while still saying close to the safety of the shore.

Walk along the promenade above Meadfoot beach with the beach huts to your right. For years this has been a popular swimming place in Torbay; indeed in 1900 it became the first place in the resort to allow mixed bathing; very daring at the time. It feels like the Medi-

terranean, with its arc of blue sea and its pine trees. Add a glamorous open top car gliding by along the beachside road on a sunny day, and you could actually be on the French, not the English Riviera.

At the end of the promenade there is the unmissable looming mass of Triangle Point. It juts out, a solid geometrical block of rock. This is the starting point for the swim. Enter the water via the helpfully placed steps to the left of Triangle Point, and swim around the Triangle, heading right, away from the beach, pausing to admire the rock's dramatic striations. The rock is made of middle Devonian limestone, and is a fossilised coral reef; look out for people fishing from here.

Continue swimming and to your right you will see massed red and grey rock. This is Knoll Quarry, where gold was found in the nineteenth century; it's thought there are still traces there. (Don't get excited, the amounts are minimal). Ahead, off the shore, you will see West Shag Rock. As you approach it, you're likely to see resident cormorants perched on top. You can usually get quite close before they fly away.

West Shag, like all the outcrops of rock on

this swim, might make you slightly giddy as its folds come at a sideways angle to the sea. It's a reminder of the earth's huge tectonic plate movements which forced the rock into dramatic shapes millions of years ago. London Bridge, a rock arch slightly further on, is another extreme example.

Swim up to West Shag and touch it to 'claim it' before heading back towards the shore, where you'll see a huge cliff fall. This dates from the nineteenth century and apparently gives the area its name, Daddyhole. The fall was supposed to be the work of the Devil – and Daddy is an old Devonian word for the

Devil. Another legend has it that the "Daddy" lived in a hole at the bottom of the cliff, which you will see as you swim a little further on, towards the harbour.

Keep hugging the shoreline and notice the colour of the water. It is particularly concentrated next to the rocky shore. Depending on how sunny a day it is, you will notice how the green or blue of the sea intensifies the closer you get to the rock. There are lots of barnacle-covered areas, which look beautifully pale underwater.

Next you pass a couple of rocks just offshore called the Magwintons; they sit astride

what's known as "Jim Davidson's Reef" by local sailors. This was after the well-known and controversial comedian who apparently ran his boat aground there after a little too much partying.

Keep swimming towards the harbour and you will come along to the Devil's Cave – known variously as Daddy Hole and Thunder Hole. While we were on a 'seafari' on a local boat, the commentator described how this rock formation was created millions of years ago as a result of volcanic activity, and pointed out the scorching on the rocks that's still there today. Incredibly, it really does look as though it's only just had contact with the fire and heat. The 'Thunder Hole' name apparently comes from the crashing sound of the sea swelling within the cave. The sound is really awesome, and rather chilling.

At this point it's time to turn back. If you're tired, you can head back the way you came, hugging the coastline. However, for a longer swim, it is fun, once you've passed West Shag Rock, to swim out to East Shag Rock, a little further out to sea directly off the main beach. Although this is its name on the map, most locals call it simply Shag Rock. It is quite a bit bigger than West Shag, but is similar looking, with stark folds of rock at an angle to the water. The famous author, Agatha Christie, who grew up in Torquay, often swam at Meadfoot, and used to enjoy the challenge of swimming out to the islands, so you are in good company!

As you swim back to shore, you will notice an arched opening in the sea wall under the hotel. This was apparently built for the lady guests, so they could get from the hotel to the sea without being bothered by beggars or other riff raff on the way.

As you get out, you can imagine Darwin living here, gazing out at the sea, and putting the finishing touches to his theory of evolution. It's also interesting to ponder on the Aquatic Ape theory, which emerged over a hundred years later. The theory – which is controversial - argues that at some point in our evolution we were water-based animals. Whether or not it is right, it would certainly perhaps give a clue as to why some of us at least feel our natural place is in the sea.

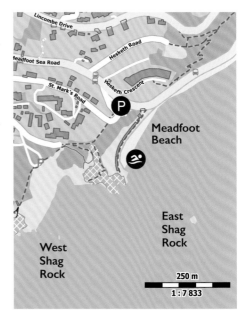

INFORMATION

SWIM ROUTE: Enter the water from the western end of the beach, at the far end of the row of beach huts. (There are steps down). Swim south past Triangle Rock on your right, and then turn right, hugging the coastline. You will see West Shag Rock ahead, swim up to it and then continue west, with the shore on your right, to find the Magwintons and Thunderhole Cave. At this point you can turn around and swim back the way you came, or extend the swim. To do this, once past West Shag Rock continue on to East Shag Rock which you will see over to the east. From East Shag Rock, swim directly back to the beach.

DISTANCE: 1 mile (the full circuit;

if you omit East Shag Rock it is a little shorter).

BEST TIDE STATE: It doesn't really matter, but it's a good idea to swim at slack water (either high or low) as the movement of the water is at its slowest.

SWIM HIGHLIGHT: The islands

GET OUT POINTS: There aren't really any, you could hang on to Triangle Rock if you needed a rest

POTENTIAL HAZARDS: There are quite a few boats passing by, particularly in the summer, so it is strongly advised that you wear a bright swim cap and a towfloat. Also look out for jetskis.

DOGS: Not allowed between 1 May and 30 September.

PARKING: Free on Meadfoot Sea Road. TQ1 2LL, SX 930 630, what3words: wisdom.slimy.nasal

PUBLIC TRANSPORT: The 64 bus from Castle Circus in Torquay stops at Meadfoot Sea Road.

REFRESHMENTS: Meadfoot Beach Café is open all year rounds and serves a range of hot tasty snacks as well as cakes and ice creams 01803 213988. For a treat you could try afternoon tea at the Osborne Hotel, just above the beach 01803 213311.

EASIER ACCESS: Parking is right by the beach. It's a very short walk onto the promenade above the water, and there are concrete steps down to the beach.

LONDON BRIDGE AND ITS CAVES

A dramatic swim to one of Torquay's most amazing natural landmarks. Swim at low tide to see the full extent of the caves

The stunning natural arch of London Bridge in Torquay is one of nature's finest sculptures and swimming through it is a fun and fascinating challenge. You can do the swim at any state of the tide, but it's important to understand the relative advantages and disadvantages of this bit of coast at both high and low water.

It is very rocky, so at high tide you will be able to glide over all the rocks and there won't be any floundering about in shallow water. You will be able to swim under the arch and through to the other side, enjoying the spectacular views. However, you won't be able to explore the 'swim-through' tunnels and caves under the arch, which are covered up at high tide, and you won't get to see the interesting sea sponges and corals that are exposed at low water. Doing the swim at low tide means you will still be able to swim through the arch, but you will also be able to explore the swim-through caves. However, you may have to put up with a bit of shallow water and rock scrambling at the beginning of the swim.

The adventure starts at Peaked Tor Cove, just past the Imperial Hotel on the South West coast path. To get down to the beach, you walk down around 150 steps, through the sadly now rather scruffy Mediterranean-style terraces, towards an old military pillbox. Apparently, in the Second World War, a string of underwater mines led from this mine watcher's post all the way over to Hollicombe. If the Germans had tried to invade, sentries could wind in a cable that would release the mines, allowing them to float to the surface. Don't worry, all the mines were recovered after the war. The old pill box is now the secure roost for a colony of greater horseshoe bats.

Peaked Tor Cove is a small, rocky beach, which was designated as a gentlemen's bathing cove in the late 19th century. The nearest ladies' beach was Beacon Cove, a safe distance away from men (but not from the caddish eyes of voyeurs using opera glasses in the window of the Royal Torbay Yacht Club). You will see a large concrete platform over the water which used to be fondly known as the 'slab'. In its heyday it had a diving board as well as a little shed, and old photos show it packed with sunbathers and swimmers. Unfortunately, it is now in a state of disrepair, but you can still use the semi-eroded steps to get into the water, or else swim directly off the beach.

Looking out to sea, you will see Saddle Rock (also known as Scrap Rock) on the left, an imposing limestone sea stack rising out of the waters, with two distinctive trademark fingers of stone on top. To your right there are two other prominent islets called The Millstones, with Living Coasts, a coastal zoo, (sadly now closed) behind. Looking back towards land, steep woods of holm oak cling precariously to the limestone cliffs.

Saddle Rock has been the scene of some amazing diving exploits over the years. If you were to climb to the top you would find a small concrete platform. This was created by local diving legend Tack Collins back at the beginning of the twentieth century. He used the rock to practise for the 1908 Olympic high diving team (there is a photo of him diving from the rock at the beginning of the book).

His obituary is quite remarkable:

"Frank Collings (1872-1950). With no public baths available in the area, Collings - nicknamed 'Tack' originally 'Tacker' on account of his small stature - taught himself to dive, plunging from rocks into the open sea. A founder member of Torquay Leander, he raised funds for the swimming club with exhibitions of trick diving featuring his speciality - the daring 'Monte Cristo'. The feat required the diver to have his hands and feet bound,

before being placed in a tied sack which was dropped from the diving stage. 'Tack' then freed himself underwater in the manner of renowned escapologist 'Houdini'. During the celebrations for Queen Victoria's Diamond Jubilee in 1897, 'Tack' thrilled a huge crowd on Princess Pier by making a 100-foot dive passing through a barrel then performing a double somersault before making a perfect entry into a depth of only fifteen feet of water."

He obviously started a trend, because, around thirty years later, in 1933, three girls were filmed doing graceful swallow dives from the very same spot. You can see the spectacular footage on the British Pathe website; the film is called Taking A Chance and is well worth a look. It would seem that Torquay was once the Acapulco of the British Isles!

The swim route takes you past Saddle Rock, and along the coast, passing the site of an old quarry, to London Bridge. From the beach, swim to your left and out around Saddle Rock. (At high water you can take a short cut, swimming over the rocks to the left of Saddle Rock, but the rest of the time you will need to swim around the outside of it). Once past the rock, you will soon see a large flattish area on your left, carved into the cliffs. This is known as Dyer's Quarry; several limestone quarries like this one can be found around the Bay. The stone taken from them was used to build many of the town's civic buildings (as well as those annoyingly high kerbstones that you always managed to scrape your tyres on when parking).

The Quarry became a site of special scientific interest in 1988, due to the prolific fossils discovered during quarrying. Dating back to the Devonian period, fossils of corals and other fauna can be found trapped in time. The area is fascinating to geologists, as these examples were fossilised in their position of growth on the seabed around 400 million years ago.

The quarry is popular with young cliff jumpers or 'tombstoners' who have nicknames for many of the jumps in the area, mostly inspired by burgers including "Big Mac" and "Hamburger Hill." The quarry face and floor also boast a colourful variety of flora including

rock samphire and the attractively named scurvy weed (both edible), as well as yellow flowers from the Mediterranean, brought back by Victorian plant hunters, which escaped from the gardens of their villas.

Your goal of London Bridge should be completely in view by now. It is a famous landmark that has been the subject of countless photos, paintings and postcards dating back over the past 100 years. The rock arch was originally part of the ocean floor. Layers of sediments built up and then, as a result of continental drift and all of the folding and faulting during the Carboniferous period, these layers were pushed up so they are almost vertical. Some eroded and fell away, leaving the harder layers of rock to form the bridge. In time, the top section will also fall away leaving two stacks; nature has a way of destroying her own sculptures to form new ones.

No one knows quite how the arch got its name. There has been much speculation over the years, and certainly, there was a trend in the nineteenth century in Torquay to name certain streets, for example Pimlico and Grosvenor, after places in London, to impress tourists. But it's thought the name has been in use for much longer than that; perhaps it is a reference to the nursery rhyme "London Bridge is falling down"? The rock is most certainly vulnerable to erosion.

The approach to the arch from the water is spectacular. The huge form towers above you, and it feels exciting to swim under its massive structure. Be careful, there is a rock directly under the arch, which may or may not be covered with water, depending on the state of the tide. At high water, you can swim over it and through the arch and round to the other side, where there are two caves.

At low tide, there is an absolutely amazing 'swim through' tunnel, which is on the left as you go under the arch from Peaked Tor Cove. Swim in, and you will see two passageways. In the right conditions, the water is an intense turquoise, because of the way the light is refracted by the cave walls. You can see sea sponges, including grey elephant-hide sponge, and masses of dead men's fingers (a type of soft coral), glowing white underwater. There are also colourful anemones, including bright pink jewel anemones, and, if you're really

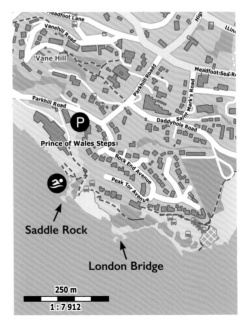

lucky, you might see starfish on the cave walls. On one occasion we saw hundreds and hundreds of them clinging to the rock faces around the arch.

Beyond London Bridge, if you keep swimming to the left, you will find another sea cave which is accessible at most states of the tide. It is a large one, and it feels as though you are entering a sort of watery cathedral; it is magnificent.

Of course, the real reward is swimming through the arch itself, a stunning natural creation millions of years in the making. If you have brought goggles, take a look at the amazing geology and marine life below the surface. And make sure you take the time and pause to look up above you – don't worry, the chances of London Bridge falling down at precisely the moment you are under it are extremely slim!

INFORMATION

SWIM ROUTE: Enter the water from Peaked Tor Cove and head to the left (south) and swim around Saddle Rock. Continue south east, with the shore on your left, past Dyer's Quarry until you reach London Bridge. Once under the arch, you have various options, depending on the tide. If it's high, continue through the arch and bear left, following the coastline, to find first a channel and then a cave you can swim into. If it's low, once under the arch you will find a tunnel to your left that you can swim through into a cave on the other side. You can also of course continue under the arch and explore the caves from the other side. Return to the beach the way you came.

DISTANCE: 0.5 miles.

BEST TIDE STATE: To explore the swim-through cave under the arch, you need to swim at low water; this should also enable you to see the corals, anemones and sea sponges that live on the cave walls

(for best wildlife viewing you need a low spring tide). The swim can also be done at other states of the tide although you won't be able to experience the swim-through cave.

SWIM HIGHLIGHT: London Bridge Natural Arch.

GET OUT POINTS: There aren't really any, you could hang on to Saddle Rock if you needed a rest.

POTENTIAL HAZARDS: There are often people fishing from Dyer's Quarry on the route to London Bridge, so look out for their lines. There are often boats in the area too, so it is strongly advised that you wear a bright swim cap and a tow float. Caves can be dangerous in rough seas; only go under the arch and in the caves if the conditions are calm.

DOGS: Allowed all year round.

PARKING: Either paying car park at Beacon Quay TQI 2BG, SX 918 631, what3words finely.librarian. rare – then walk to the Imperial

Hotel and take the coast path to Peaked Tor Cove. Alternatively, park for free at Daddyhole Plain TQI 2EF, SX 926 628, what3words hogs.likes.jolly, and take the coast path to Peaked Tor Cove (about 10 minutes' walk).

PUBLIC TRANSPORT: Various buses stop at Torquay Harbour, including the Number 12. From the harbour, it is a short walk to Peaked Tor Cove.

REFRESHMENTS: Below Decks is at nearby Beacon Quay, overlooking the harbour and serves seafood including moule frites, as well as jacket potatoes and sandwiches. 01803 411106. Rockfish on Victoria Parade does traditional fish and chips. 01803 212175.

EASIER ACCESS: Peaked Tor Cove is not that accessible. From the nearest car park, it is about 10 minutes' walk, and then you have to descend around 150 steps to get to the beach which is rocky.

Swim 7

BEACON COVE
AND THE MILLSTONES

A lovely swim from one of Torquay's most central beaches, to nearby Peaked Tor Cove, taking in two islets on the way

This short but fascinating swim is particularly good fun, as it takes you from what was once the Ladies' Bathing Cove, past the Imperial Hotel to the former Gentlemen's Bathing Beach at Peaked Tor Cove and back again. This little watery jaunt certainly would never have been tolerated during the frosty and frumpy Victorian era and the authors of this book wouldn't have been allowed to swim together, even for research purposes.

There were four dedicated ladies' places, including here at Beacon Cove, which is the resort's oldest recorded bathing facility. The men had one up on the women, with five bathing areas including Torre Abbey Sands, Livermead and the facilities at Peaked Tor Cove. Beacon Cove was actually one of the first beaches to boast bathing machines in South Devon and after paying 6d (six pence) for the first half hour and 6d for each additional quarter of an hour, women were provided with 'proper' bathing costumes and two towels.

It was a popular swimming spot for a young Agatha Christie who describes both the beach and the eight colourfully striped bathing machines in loving detail in her captivating autobiography. The idea was that a lady would bolt herself inside the box on wheels to get changed, then the contraption was lowered down to the water so she could enter the sea with her modesty intact.

An elderly attendant would release the bathing machines without warning; the result being that the cubicle would begin bumping down the steep beach and over rocks and stones, sending the passengers flying. However, despite all of the precautions, it would seem that the Ladies Bathing Place wasn't quite as safe from prying eyes as the modest Victorian women may have liked.

As Agatha explains, 'The Torbay Yacht Club was stationed on Beacon Terrace, just above the Ladies' Bathing Cove, and although the beach was properly invisible from the club windows, the sea around the raft was not, and, according to my father, a good many of the gentlemen spent their time with opera glasses enjoying the sight of female figures displayed in what they hopefully thought of as almost a state of nudity! I don't think we can have been very appealing in those shapeless garments. The Gentlemen's Bathing Cove was situated further along the coast. There the gentlemen, in their scanty triangles, could disport themselves as much as they pleased, with no female eye able to observe them from any point whatever.'

On the beach, it's worth pausing and looking around to get your bearings. Behind you, you'll be able to see the Royal Torbay Yacht Club, and on the right, looming above the cove, is a site that used to be the home of a coastal zoo called Living Coasts. An outpost of Paignton Zoo, it originally opened in 2003 and was home to many creatures including penguins, puffins, fur seals, ducks and avocets. Sadly though, after the pandemic in 2020 it never re-opened, although there are plans afoot for its future use.

The swim route starts on the right-hand side of the beach; you pass alongside the old Living Coasts site which has a fascinating and, at times, tragic past, and is a kind of microcosm of the history of public sea swimming and recreation. In the sea wall you will see old bricks that once formed part of the Assembly Rooms, which later, in the 1850s, became the Bath Saloons, and was then renamed the Marine Spa. This was a large, grand building with sun terraces designed for people to take full advantage of the sea.

A saltwater swimming pool was built here in 1914, while in 1924 a ballroom was opened in an area that had variously been used as

a palm court, skating rink and badminton court. A Vitiglass sun-lounge was created at the end of the 1920s and extended to cover most of the seaward side of the building a few years later. Patrons could experience all manner of therapies including seaweed baths, and even, apparently, the Dartmoor Peat Pack Treatment.

With spectacular views, the Marine Spa was used as the headquarters for the 1948 Olympics, when the sailing races were held in Torquay. In the 1950s the Torquay Leander Swimming Club performed its famous water ballets there, with synchronised swimming by champion girl swimmers, all set to music in an Esther Williams style.

However, in 1971, a young boy called John Moran tragically died in the spa, after being sucked down a drainage pipe. (Appallingly, there had been a similar incident a few decades earlier, when the same thing had happened to a young girl, who did, miraculously survive). Amid the scandal, the building was demolished that same year. There is a small plaque remembering John on the wall alongside the path leading down to Beacon Cove.

After a few years lying empty, an entertainments complex called Coral Island opened on the site in 1977, which at first seemed like an exciting new development, with discos, slot machines, bars, and even wrestling. However, it struggled to attract customers outside the summer months and started to fall into decline. In 1988 it closed, and the building

became derelict. For around a decade this prominent site at the heart of Torquay's waterfront was boarded up, vandalised and unloved, and it came to symbolise the town's decline as a tourist resort, and indeed, the demise of the British seaside holiday. At the time of writing, there is once again a question mark over this superb coastal site. Fingers crossed something good is built there.

Swim a little further out in the direction of the two islets which are called the Millstones, and at low tide you'll be able to see a line of boulders reaching out to these natural landmarks. This was once a stone pier that was swept away in the great storm of 1859. To your right is the great arm of Haldon Pier, which was built a few years later in 1867, and created a new, outer harbour for Torquay. The stone to build the pier was quarried from nearby Beacon Hill.

Haldon Pier helps provide protection not just for the boats, but for a large area of sea grass beds which grow here, which is about the size of twelve football pitches, starting just five to ten metres from the shore. Seagrass isn't a type of seaweed but is a flowering plant, with long grass-like leaves that form dense meadows; it is the only plant able to live in seawater and pollinate while submerged. The beds are home to a diverse community of animals, including seahorses, pipefish, crabs, prawns, lobsters, and cuttlefish. They are also breeding grounds for cuttlefish and sharks, and nurseries for cod, plaice and pollock.

Seagrass meadows also have the potential to store large amounts of carbon; in fact, they capture carbon at a rate 35 times faster than tropical rainforests. There are five meadows in Torbay: here, in Millstones Bay, Breakwater Beach in Brixham, Elberry Cove, Churston Cove and between Livermead and Torre Abbey Sands. There is now action being taken to protect them; boats are not allowed to anchor in these areas, which are marked by special seagrass buoys.

Turn left, swimming away from the Mill Stones, towards the Imperial Hotel. To your left, on the edge of Beacon Cove, you will see some stone steps carved into the cliffs. There was once a popular long wooden diving board here, sadly now lost to erosion and health and safety fears. The Royal Naval Lifeboat Institution built a station on Beacon Cove back in 1875. A series of lifeboats were launched from here over the years, powered by oars and some very brave men. The last boat to operate from the beach was the Wighton, but this was retired in 1922 when new vessels were introduced in Brixham. The station operated as a cafe for many years and is sorely missed.

Swim with the shoreline on your left and in the direction of Saddle Rock, which has two fingers of rock on its summit, which seem to break free from the natural sculpture like a huge crab's claw. You are now swimming along the limestone cliff that forms the natural garden wall of the Imperial Hotel.

The hotel was built on the site of two former villas, The Cove and The Cliff and opened by the Torquay Hotel Company in 1866, which declared: 'It has long been felt that Torquay, with a large, wealthy and increasing popula-

tion, and great numbers of visitors who resort to it in both winter and summer for health and pleasure, stands much in need of the accommodation of a first-class modern hotel of the character so successfully established in London and some of the leading watering places of England and the continent.'

The hotel has welcomed many famous guests over the years including Emperor Napoleon III, the Queen of the Netherlands, Benjamin

Disraeli, Henry Kissinger and Agatha Christie, who enjoyed dinner and dances at what was at the time one of the most glamorous hotels in the UK. The hotel features in three of her mysteries including *Peril at End House*, (where it becomes The Majestic) and *Sleeping Murder*, where Miss Marple solves the crime on the hotel terrace.

The hotel was given a new facade in the 1960's and while not as visually appealing as it once was, the huge white building still looks impressive as you swim by, with the trees and greenery of the gardens hanging over the limestone cliffs, giving it a Mediterranean feel. As you follow the 'layer cake' tide line on the face of the cliffs, look out for a small hidden cove carved into the cliffs below the hotel. This was once a boat landing and you can still see the steps leading up to the hotel.

This mysterious little cove, which looks like something straight out of a Famous Five book, would also have been the perfect place to discreetly arrive at the hotel. When the royal Yacht Britannia was anchored in the Bay, Edward VII (then the Prince of Wales) would be ferried over to these steps, so he could slip upstairs to a suite where his mistress, Lillie Langtry, would be waiting.

The turnaround point for the swim is the beach at Peaked Tor Cove, unless you wish to extend the swim to include London Bridge Arch (as described in the previous chapter). If the weather is nice you might want to have a rest and dry off in the sun on the concrete terrace above. There was once a small shed here, as described by W Miller in *Our English Shores*, an 1888 book on English Resorts:

'When living at the Imperial Hotel I bathed before breakfast from a little shed erected on the shore nearly below the hotel for the convenience of bathers who can swim. The air (at 7 a.m.) was then cold but the water was warm. No charge was made for the shed, but two pence (was charged) if a box shut in by a door were used.'

In later years the hotel would erect a row of square-shaped canvas tents there; small metal rings used to secure them can still be seen in the concrete. It's hard to imagine that this place once attracted hundreds of men-only swimmers throughout the year. Mixed bathing was finally allowed in 1900, thanks to the efforts of a group of people led by Ernest Hutchings, who later became the Torquay Coroner.

As you swim back to Beacon Cove, we'd like to leave you with Agatha Christie's playful recollections of the controversy at the time:

'A pathetic tale was told of the Council Meeting at which the question of mixed bathing came up for final approval. A very old Councillor, a vehement opponent, finally defeated, quavered out his last plea: "And all I say is, Mr. Mayor, if this 'ere mixed bathing is carried through, that there will be decent partitions in the bathing machines, however low."'

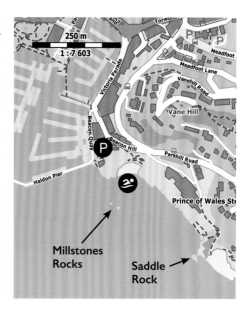

INFORMATION

SWIM ROUTE: From the beach, swim out alongside the right-hand-side of the cove, towards Haldon Pier. Swim up to the Millstones, and then head left over towards the Imperial Hotel. At the eastern end of Beacon Cove look out for the old stone steps leading down into the water, where there used to be a diving board. Continue swimming with the shore on your left, past the Imperial Hotel and its hidden cove. Arrive at Peaked Tor Cove and get out for a rest if you fancy, before swimming back the way you came.

DISTANCE: 0.5 miles.

BEST TIDE STATE: It doesn't really matter. The top half of the tide is better, as the beach is rocky.

SWIM HIGHLIGHT: The Millstones.

GET OUT POINTS: The hidden cove under the Imperial Hotel.

POTENTIAL HAZARDS: This is a pretty quiet area where there are not many boats, but it's always a good idea to wear a brightly coloured cap and a tow float.

DOGS: Allowed all year round.

PARKING: Car park at Beacon Quay TQ1 2BG, SX 918 631, what3words finely.librarian.rare

PUBLIC TRANSPORT: Various buses stop at Torquay Harbour,

including the number 12 which serves Newton Abbot, Torquay, Paignton and Brixham. From the harbour, it is a short walk to Beacon Cove.

REFRESHMENTS: The Elephant is a Michelin-starred restaurant very close to Beacon Cove, which is friendly and informal. 01803 200044. The long-established Number 7 Fish Bistro specialises in seafood 01803 295055.

EASIER ACCESS: Beacon Cove is right near the car park: park on the top deck. From there it is a short walk down a slope to the beach, which is uneven and rocky.

CORBYN HEAD AND ITS CAVES

A gorgeous swim out around a sandstone headland, past a sequence of intriguing caves

When viewed from the spectacular lookout at the summit of Rock Walk in Torquay, the two headlands of Corbyn Head and Livermead Cliff seem to curl around Livermead Bay, resembling a crab sculpted in clay by the hands of a child. Or a slightly mouldy croissant. This swim takes you from Corbyn Beach (once known as Chelston Beach) at the far western End of Torre Abbey Sands, around this striking headland, riddled with amazing caves carved by the relentless sea into the red clay and sandstone.

The swim starts at Corbyn Beach, from the sands of the tiny cove, overlooked by a charming line of colourful beach huts and the striking Victorian and Art Deco magnificence of The Grand Hotel. Agatha Christie spent her honeymoon here and the venue forms part of the Agatha Christie Mile, taking in many landmarks and locations from the author's life and works. Agatha also took Corbyn Head as her inspiration for Baldy's Head in her novel *Postern of Fate*. It's also worth remembering at the end of your swim that Jacob's Creek voted the hotel as being one of the 20 best views in the world to enjoy a glass of wine!

It's best to do this swim on a fairly high tide, as there are lots of rocks off Corbyn Beach and at low tide, lots of quite pongy seaweed, which certainly detracts from the romanticism of owning a beach hut here. Apparently, a few years ago, some bright spark, rumoured to work for the Grand Hotel, had the idea of concreting in the rock pools as a way of getting rid of the smell. Fortunately, this idea never saw the light of day.

Having said that, it's worth checking the area out at a low tide one day, as you can see the remains of an old quay, where goods were almost certainly brought in for the Abbots and Canons at nearby Torre Abbey. Nick Pannell suggests in his book "Torbay – The History and Wildlife of Torbay's Dramatic Shoreline" that everything from French wine to papal emissaries would have landed here, as well as the Spanish prisoners captured during the Armada, who were then imprisoned in the Spanish Barn in front of the Abbey buildings.

Enter the water from the right hand side of the beach, and swim with the shore on your right. You'll see a large shark fin-shaped red rock on your right, separated from the cliffs, capped with a punk hairstyle of green foliage. This was once much larger and sheltered an old boat yard, but the sea has worked relentlessly to chisel away the rock and to carve the many sea caves that will soon come into view. You'll also notice a warning sign that explains that the cliffs around the corner get cut off by the tide. Not a problem for wild swimmers, but a perpetual issue for young teenage boys.

Corbyn Head (formally known as Corbyn's Head) was given to the council back in 1907 by the Mallock family, then owners of Cockington and Chelston. Legend has it that the headland was named after one Samuel Corbyn, a south west pirate who was hanged on gallows built on the headland. Most of the trees shown on old postcards of the once wooded Corbyn Head were sadly lost to Dutch Elm Disease, although a group of fir trees remains.

You'll notice some curious colours in the cliffs resembling streaky bacon. Continuing past a collapsed cave, even more amazing colour palettes are introduced – multiple shades of brown and terracotta and pastel pinks and orange. Further on, the cliffs above you really hint at their desert origins, as if you are floating through a flooded Arizona valley with canyon walls above. It's only the fertile greens topping the cliffs that remind you are in a more lush European country.

Yet again, man's ever-futile battle with nature is very evident in the cliffs here, with impressive brick walls still plugging many of the holes. In the past, many elaborate plans to prevent further erosion have been suggested, including extending Corbyn Head to create a car park, or the completely dangerous and insane/bold and imaginative plan (delete as applicable) to build a Torquay Airport on the headland back in 1934.

Old photographs show that a pyramid-shaped natural arch called Mitre Rock once stood beside the headland, with a tunnel to clamber through in the middle. Sadly, this popular tourist attraction collapsed during the middle of the last century, leaving a large number of rocks below the surface here. You can still see the coastal defence walls which used to double as a pathway so that people could walk around the corner and through the various sea caves to enjoy views over Livermead decades ago.

During the Second World War the headland was used as the town's main coastal battery, with huge guns in place to defend Torquay from coastal invasion. While the guns were never fired in anger, six men lost their lives here in 1944 when a training exercise went disastrously wrong and a shell exploded. A touching memorial to the men can be found on the headland.

Interestingly, another suggestion for the origin of the name Corbyn is that it is a corruption of the 12th-century term coryvanesse, meaning the "carved nose." And as you round the corner, that exactly what the headland looks like, a sculpted nose or even slightly reptilian-shaped face. You'll also notice more remarkable lines of colours in the sandstone, showing the layered history of the cliffs, readable like rings in a carved tree.

As you swim further around you may see a secret beach, the legendary goal of many a young adventurer. Swim into this natural

amphitheatre, pause and listen. The sea makes an amplified sound as it groans and gurgles and relentlessly explores the submerged passages and channels through the headland. You'll also see the first of the sea caves high up in the cliff, with the wall and former walkway below.

In the early 20th century, there was a plan to turn Torquay into a sort of British Hollywood, and Corbyn's Head was used as the location for an early silent film called The Rocks of Valpre, based on a novel by Ethel M Dell. As Kevin Dixon explains in his series of online articles called Torquay's Other History:

"The novel begins in a 'Magic Cave' on a 'rocky coast' and Corbyn Head was an ideal location. The storyline has a young English woman walking on the beach of the French town of Valpre when she falls and injures her ankle. A young Frenchman comes to her

rescue and invites her back to his cave to see a 'magic secret'. This turns out to be a new gun he is inventing. The tide comes in and they are cut off, meaning they have to spend the night together. Back in Valpre, rumours spread and the gun inventor finds himself challenged to a duel. This duel is fought on Corbyn Head just behind the public toilets. As the men fence, the heroine stares towards the Marine Spa. It ends with a romantic scene on Rock Walk where the couple promise to love each other."

Another large cave can be discovered further along and it is possible to carefully scramble up over the concrete wall to look inside. This cave fills up with water through a hidden entrance as the tide comes in and is certainly atmospheric. Back in the sea and a series of more caves and natural chambers come into view, an incredible hidden world unseen by the people enjoying the park above. This is one of the areas of Torbay where the council have decided to allow erosion to continue unchallenged, allowing even more of these amazing caves to form.

The swim ends as Livermead Beach comes into view, although it is mostly covered up at high tide. It is possible to exit at the steps in the sea wall about half way along the beach, although we would recommend returning the way you came, which offers stunning views towards Torquay harbour and the marina. Look out for stranded teenagers along the way and resist the urge to move into one of the caves and wait for some romance to come your way. Don't forget there is wine with a view waiting for you back on shore.

INFORMATION

SWIM ROUTE: From Corbyn Head beach, swim out to sea with the headland on your right. Hug the headland and follow it round to the right, swimming past the caves and old walls on your right. Continue on to Livermead Beach where you turn round and swim back the way you came.

DISTANCE: 0.4 miles.

BEST TIDE STATE: Mid to high tide.

SWIM HIGHLIGHT:
Caves at Corbyn Head.

GET OUT POINTS: Steps in sea wall at Livermead.

POTENTIAL HAZARDS: Exposed rocks, so it is a good idea to wear swim shoes. Fortunately the area is fairly free of boat traffic especially if you stay close to the shore. A bright swim cap and tow float is always advised.

DOGS: Allowed all year round.

PARKING: Meters on Torbay Road TQ2 6NX SX 907 634 what3words rested.stores.elder

PUBLIC TRANSPORT: The 12 bus stops on Torbay Road.

REFRESHMENTS: The Corbyn Head Beach Café is open in the summer months. No phone number. For a treat, why not try afternoon tea at the Grand Hotel 01803 296677.

EASIER ACCESS: Parking is very close to the beach, and access into the water (especially at high tide) is fairly easy.

Corbyn Beach

Caves

Livermead Beach

250 m

1 : 7 991

Swim 9

LIVERMEAD HEAD
AND THE HINDU TEMPLES

A very special swim around an atmospheric headland
with an astonishing chain of swim-through caves

This amazing swim starts near Institute Beach next to the Livermead Cliff Hotel (easy to spot as the establishment's name is not so subtly marked in white paint on the seawalls below) and takes you right around to Hollicombe Beach past an unusual set of sea caves. It is thought that the name Livermead comes from the Anglo Saxon 'laefer' (or lefer) meaning a wild iris, bullrush or reed, and 'mead' meaning meadow, and has nothing to do with the damage drinking too much mead could do to your liver.

The Livermead Cliff Hotel stands on the former site of Livermead Cottage, which was erected in 1825 and became a lodging house before being gutted by fire in January 1886. Livermead Cliff House was built in 1905 and opened as a hotel in 1922. An advert from the time described it as being "The Premier Private Hotel. The only hotel directly on the sea front with private boat landing and bathing platform."

The advert also boasted of 'separate tables', 'electric light', 'fitted hot and cold water' and 'lavatory basins.' In a curious turn of fate, the hotel's salt water heated swimming pool, which opened in 1990, was filled in following government regulations concerning the depth of pools and the need to have a lifeguard always on duty. It's now a rather nice sun deck called The Riviera Terrace and a great spot for a brew with a view.

The little sandy stretch next to the hotel is called Institute Beach. It was owned by the Mallock family (who owned the manors of Cockington and Chelston a little way inland), who handed it over to the council in 1920 on two conditions: that they could take between 2 and 15 loads of sand from the beach each year and that they could erect their own bathing tent there. The millstones in Cockington were also carved from rock taken from this beach, while you'll also be able to see the stream from Cockington flowing out to the right of the hotel, which used to power a watermill.

At a low tide the foundation stones of the arm of a medieval harbour, carved from the surrounding rocks become visible, extending from Livermead Head. A second quay can also be seen stretching out from Livermead Sands. Local historian Kevin Dixon says old records from the fourteenth century show that permission was given for the Canons of

Torre Abbey to fish with nets at Livermead. And this might give a clue as to the beach's unusual name. Apparently, when monks receive the order of the priesthood, it's referred to as institute.

Fishing carried on here for hundreds of years; several cottages and fish cellars are depicted in a drawing dated 1661. And the harbour would have been where goods for Cockington Court would have been delivered.

The swim route goes out from Institute Beach and around Livermead Head, and on towards Hollicombe. It is best done at high tide, so you can swim through the caves. At the time of writing, the usual access to the beach, from steps on Cliff Road, is blocked with a barrier, although some people manage to squeeze past it. There are also some steps down to the water from on the other side of the hotel. Go through the gate for the beer garden (from the hotel car park) and make your way down. If the gate is locked, you could also enter the water from steps in the sea wall at Livermead Beach.

Once in the water, bear right towards Livermead Head. As you get nearer the cliffs at Institute Beach, you might see old sections of brick wall lying around; evidence of man's futile attempts at stopping the relentless erosion of the sandstone cliffs. Also notice the horizontal layers in the rocks, built up over the centuries during the desert conditions

millions of years ago, and now being sculpted by majestic hand of the sea.

Hug the coast on your right and swim around the corner of the headland (there is a large rock platform here where you can get out and rest if you need to). You will start to see an extraordinary series of arched sea caverns in the Permian rock, which we dubbed the Hindu Temples after reading a description by Charles Kingsley.

The author of *The Water Babies* spent the winter of 1853 in Torquay with his wife while she recovered from a miscarriage. Renting Livermead House from Charles Mallock,

they spent many happy hours exploring the coast of the local area. Kingsley even wrote a book about it, called *Glaucus: or the Wonders of the Shore* which was published in 1855 and become an instant best seller, reprinted several times over.

Here's his wonderful description of the amazing red caves at this location:

"Follow us, then, reader, in imagination, out of the gay watering place [Torquay] with its London shops and London equipages, along the broad road beneath the sunny limestone cliffs, tufted with golden furze; past the huge oaks and green slopes of Torre Abbey; and

past the fantastic rocks of Livermead, scooped by the waves into a labyrinth of double and triple caves, like Hindu temples, upborn on pillars banded with yellow and white and red, a week's study, in form and colour and chiaroscuro, for any artist."

For many years these incredible caves were largely forgotten, despite being in the middle of Torbay. And yet, in Victorian times, these caves were a real attraction. Charles Kingsley, as a visitor, was obviously aware of them. Old books about Torbay refer to them, and there is a beautiful engraving of them in one, the Torquay Pictorial of 1893 (see below).

As you explore the chambers with unique views of the sea and town framed by the curved natural windows, it's worth taking a second to enjoy this secret place only ever really visited by fellow wild swim adventurers and kayakers. Thousands of people drive past every day on the main road between Torquay and Paignton, unaware of the dramatic natural beauty of the coastline just yards away.

The first cave you get to looms magnificently, with a large arched entrance. As you swim in there is a small channel to the right which is a dead end. Bear left and you can swim out through the cave under a second archway. There is an unusual, very square cavity on the right, which looks like the top of a fireplace. The sound of the water as it echoes and rumbles around the caves is awe-inspir-

ing, as are the colours, which vary according to the time of day and the clarity of the sea.

Continue along the coast and the next set of caves is a veritable sequence of 'rooms' that we think resembles the coastal holiday retreat of the Flintstones. Depending on the height of the tide, you can swim through them all, or else you might have to do a bit of scrambling. At the far end there is a charming little hollow, like a basin or a font, that you can sit in. The caves are a wonderful place to swim at dawn. They face east, so when the sun rises, it floods them with golden light. We once had a memorable gathering here, swimming out at daybreak with champagne and smoked salmon, which we scoffed watching the sun come up.

Swim on further and you'll discover a set of steps dug into the soft stone of the cliffs, leading down from a lookout built at the end of a garden above, and on down to bathing platforms at the water's edge. It's easy to imagine swim parties being organised for guests on these exclusive rocks, followed perhaps by a few cocktails and a picnic away from the prying eyes of the masses.

The past owners of the property have tried to patch up holes being dug in the cliffs by the relentless waves, but as we know from our explorations, it's a fruitless task. One day, hopefully a long time in the future, these cliff top gardens and even the houses will become a part of the dramatic sea bed you are swimming above.

Rounding the headland, Hollicombe Beach comes into view, which is still dubbed

Gasworks Beach due to the ugly gas tanks that used to look out over the sea from this prime location until the 1960s. Today a beautiful park stands on the former site, with the beach reached through a tunnel dug in the cliffs below the railway line. Looking to your right you'll discover more steps carved into the cliff face and ahead a smaller beach called Oil Cove.

If you are making the swim during the spring and summer months, the cliffs of Livermead Head are an amazing sight, decorated by a colourful patchwork of flowers and plants that have escaped the grounds of the houses above, to form a Hanging Gardens of Hollicombe. You can now either swim back the way you came or exit the water and walk back through Hollicombe Park, and along the main coast road.

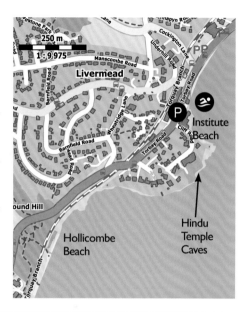

INFORMATION

SWIM ROUTE: Enter the water either from Institute Beach or from steps down from the Livermead Cliff Hotel beer garden. There is also another set of steps in the sea wall a little further on towards Corbyn Head. Swim to the right, towards Livermead Head, heading south east. Keeping the coastline on your right, follow the headland and turn the corner, away from the beach. Soon you will find the caves on your right. Continue past a flight of steps around to Hollicombe. Swim back the same way you came.

DISTANCE: 0.7 miles.

BEST TIDE STATE: High tide.

SWIM HIGHLIGHT:
The Hindu Temples.

GET OUT POINTS: There is a large rock platform at the first corner of the headland that you can rest on.

POTENTIAL HAZARDS: The cliffs here are unstable and there will always be a risk of cliff falls when you swim near caves. Use your own judgement. The area is rocky so swim shoes are a must, as is a brightly coloured swim cap and tow float. Caves can be dangerous in rough seas, so only enter if conditions are calm.

DOGS: Allowed all year round on Livermead Sands & Institute Beach.

PARKING: Free on Cliff Road: TQ2 6SW SX 903 627 what3words: legs.fault.alien

PUBLIC TRANSPORT: The 12 bus stops on Torbay Road very near the swim.

REFRESHMENTS: The Livermead Cliff Hotel does afternoon tea 01803 299666; the Blue Walnut Café in nearby Chelston does cooked breakfasts as well as various tasty snacks, and is famed for its tiny cinema. 01803 392522

EASIER ACCESS: There are steps into the sea straight from the road at Livermead Beach.

Swim 10

ROUNDHAM TO NORTH SANDS, GOODRINGTON

A fun swim taking in a tucked-away cove and a sandstone headland, and finishing at one of Paignton's loveliest beaches

Roundham Head is a charming pocket-sized headland, slap bang in the middle of Torbay, sheltered by Hope's Nose to the north, and Berry Head to the south. There is something pleasing about its smallness; you can swim around the entire headland in anything between 30 minutes to an hour, depending on your speed and how much you like to 'stop and stare'. The dramatic red weathered sandstone cliffs are fascinating, with their mysterious cracks and caves.

The swim, which is best done in the top half of the tide, to avoid rocks, starts at Fairy Cove. The beach is tucked away behind Paignton Harbour and is a bit of well-kept secret. To the left you see the massed sandstone sea wall; it was built in in the late 1830s to accommodate the town's growing trade with the rest of the world. Ahead is the pier, built in 1878; in its heyday in Victorian times, it had a billiard hall and a grand piano. It even appeared in an episode of Monty Python's Flying Circus, with John Cleese, Eric Idle, Michael Palin et al; lots of the Pythons' material was filmed in Torbay.

As you get in the water, you'll immediately notice the striking terracotta cliffs to the right of the beach. The headland is made up of a huge chunk of this Permian sandstone, created about 250-300 million years ago, when Torbay was a desert. Much of the sandstone you see at Roundham was formed by harsh winds blowing across the desert; you can see layers of the wind-blown sand in the rocks.

Swim out from the beach, heading right, keeping the cliffs on your right. The headland sits on a large reef, known as the Paignton Ledges, which stretches out underwater around it. On a low tide much of it is exposed, covered in barnacles. You will notice a black and yellow post, like a small mobile phone mast, sticking out of the sea. This is an East Cardinal Marker, which lets ships know they should stay to the East of it. Be aware that boats will be coming in and out of the harbour, but as long as you stay close to the foot of the cliffs, you'll be fine.

Swim over the reef, admiring the vast array of seaweed. There are 800 species of seaweed in the British Isles; they fall into three main categories, red, brown and green, and you can see many types of all three here. The Victorians enjoyed the challenge of identifying them so much, the pastime became known as 'seaweeding', and seaweed albums and prints became very popular. You can imagine Victorian holidaymakers, after a trip to the nearby pier, coming to this beach at low tide armed with their magnifying glasses and notebooks.

As you swim around the corner of the headland, leaving Fairy Cove behind, you get an amazing 'fish eye' view of the Bay; you can see it in its entirety, a huge semicircle of coast, with Torquay to your left, and Brixham to the right. It is spectacular. Enjoy feeling at the complete centre of it, with the water spreading out endlessly before you.

As you swim along, you'll notice what looks like a 'room' carved out of the cliff; a rectangular hole. It's a cave, but the way the cliff has eroded makes it look almost man-made. There's a little beach in front of it. This area is known as "Savage Hole", and has proved treacherous for many a ship over the years. It is named after HMS Savage, which foundered here in 1762.

Sadly, on many an occasion, the mariners' plight was made even worse by locals who took the opportunity to go down and salvage as much as possible from the wrecked ships. If you're swimming on a low tide (not advisable)

look out for a huge metallic structure, much higher than a person, sticking out of the water; it looks like an anchor and has obviously been there some time, judging by the amount of sea life attached to it.

It's fun to get out at Savage Hole, and have a quick look inside the cave. Then, as you walk out of the cave back to the sea, look at the cliffs which loom up either side of you, left and right. They look like faces in profile; the one to the left, with a very large nose, has something of the Simpsons cartoon charac-

ters about it. Once back in the water, if you continue to look at the cliffs as you swim, you will get the strange feeling that you're being watched, once you start to make out more faces in the rock.

Savage Hole is much frequented by teenagers in the summer; it's also regularly visited by the Torbay lifeboat, which often has to rescue them when they get cut off by the tide.

As you swim south, along the cliffs, look up and you'll see an attractive group of pine trees, like a lookout sentinel. They're in a little

park, Roundham Gardens, which sits atop the promontory, with benches for viewing out to sea. Give people sitting above you a wave!

The many holes and cracks in the headland are home to seabirds including of course, herring gulls, but also lesser black backed gulls and fulmars. Common pigeons like to hang out on the cliffs too; a reminder that we're still in an urban area. Also, look out for cormorants and oyster catchers. As you come around the south eastern corner – the last corner of the headland – you see the pleasure beach of Goodrington laid out before you. Still keeping the cliffs on your right, you swim alongside the grand promenade which was built in the 1920s.

In the summer, the promenade is home to colourful beach huts. Above them is a hanging garden with a zig-zagging path which leads back up to the park at the top of the promontory. Known locally by various names, including Rock Gardens, Rock Walk and Cliff Gardens, the garden contains many sub-tropical plants that were donated by Henry Whitley, the founder of Paignton Zoo.

You can get out at the soft sands of Goodrington, or else climb up the steps and out of the water onto the prom, reflecting on a journey that started at a working harbour, and finished at a family beach, passing a landscape dating back millions of years. Oh, and those faces you passed in the rock. Just how long have they been there, and what do they think as they look out to sea?

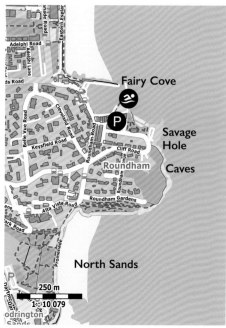

INFORMATION

SWIM ROUTE: From Fairy Cove, swim to the right, with the headland on your right. Follow it around and head south, passing the cliffs and caves of Roundham Head. Continue to hug the headland on your right, and you will then arrive at the long promenade at Goodrington North. You can get out on the main beach and walk back – in this case the swim is about half a mile. If you swim all the way back you will have swum a mile.

DISTANCE: 1 mile.

BEST TIDE STATE: It's best to swim in the top half of the tide, to avoid rocks, but the swim is possible at any state of the tide.

SWIM HIGHLIGHT: The cliffs and caves at Roundham Head.

GET OUT POINTS: There are rocks off the headland you can rest on; you can get out up steps on the promenade at North Sands, Goodrington.

POTENTIAL HAZARDS: Look out for boats; if you stay close in to the headland, you should be fine, but we strongly advise you to wear a brightly coloured swim cap and a tow float.

DOGS: Allowed all year round.

PARKING: Roundham car park, TQ4 6DH, SX 895 602, what3words treat.serve.loved

PUBLIC TRANSPORT: The 25 bus stops at Paignton near Harbour; the number 12 stops in nearby Dartmouth Road.

REFRESHMENTS: Cantina at North Sands, Goodrington is a legendary local eaterie, particularly famed for its 'crabby chips' 01803 525377; Molly's on Paignton Harbour serves snacks and drinks and often has live music 07470 510979.

EASIER ACCESS: From the car park, it's a short walk to Fairy Cove where the beach is sandy so access into the water is pretty good.

109

Swim 11

GOODRINGTON TO BROADSANDS

A swim safari through an underwater nature reserve,
passing a famous rock landmark, and finishing at a pretty beach

This is a glorious swim, because it takes you along such a constantly changing coastline, which is particularly interesting to geologists. From red cliffs to grey limestone, with outlandish shapes in the rocks, a sunken forest and a considerable length of reef, there is a lot to see. It is best done on the top half of the tide although it is still possible at low, and do wear goggles so you can see the amazing seaweeds and wildlife. The swim down to Broadsands is a mile long, so unless you fancy a long swim back, arrange to be picked up at the end.

The swim starts at the south end of Goodrington Sands, near the brightly painted beach huts and the twisting tubes of the waterpark. You start with the smell of candyfloss in your nostrils, but the bucket and spade world is soon left behind, and you find yourself immersed in nature; in fact the water you swim through is an underwater nature reserve, and the coastline between here and Broadsands is a Site of Special Scientific Interest (SSSI).

On a very low tide, it is possible to see the remains of a forest which was drowned by rising sea levels at the end of the last ice age. Look out for incongruous tree stumps in the middle of the red sand on Goodrington beach.

Goodrington, as a resort, wasn't developed until the twentieth century, unlike the main beach at Paignton which was already popular by Victorian times. Old photos show Edwardian holidaymakers at the northern end, by the red cliffs of Roundham, when it was a completely natural beach, without the built promenade we see today. The reason it may have taken a little more time to exploit Goodrington's natural assets is because for many years there was a huge marsh behind the shore. Eventually the land was reclaimed and turned into the holiday attraction you see today.

Swim south towards Brixham, keeping near the coast on your right. You may hear the hoot from the steam train; it travels right along the cliff top on its journey between Paignton and Kingswear and is a splendid sight and sound as it puffs by. The joy of this swim is that you will pass a whole series of beaches.

Generally speaking, as you swim south, you'll be going 'back in time' – at least as far as the age of the rocks is concerned. The red cliffs here are from the Permian age between two and three hundred million years ago when

Torbay was a sweltering desert. The first bay you come to is Saltern Cove; again, with red cliffs, on top of a fossilised coral reef made of Devonian limestone; the limestone is older by about a hundred million years.

The name 'saltern' refers to pools in which seaweed is left to evaporate to make salt. Saltern Cove has had several different nicknames over the years, including White Horse Beach and Monkey Pole Beach. On the headland above the cove used to be what Paigntonians nicknamed the monkey-pole. While it was widely believed to have been an ordinance lookout post, the pole with triangular wooden steps in the side was actually for firing rockets to warn ships that came too close to the shore and the dangerous rocks below. It was also used for hauling stranded people back up to their safety. Lovers would engrave their names in the pole, which was eventually moved to Berry Head.

There is a large and richly populated reef here, with a huge variety of seaweed to see. The environment is so diverse that it is designated as a local nature reserve. Unusually, the reserve extends underwater to a point 376 metres below the low water mark.

It is a magical place to snorkel when the water is calm and clear. The seaweed sways in the light as you swim over the top of it. Look out for the distinctive snakelocks anemones which are a delicate pale green with purple tips.

These anemones particularly like brightly lit, shallow water and they thrive on this reef. There are also Mermaid's Tresses, bladder wrack, saw wrack, and an amazing pink seaweed growing in clumpy blobs that looks like the pompoms hanging from your granny's lampshade - this is called Jania Rubens.

If you look out to sea you have great views from here towards Berry Head, but if you look just ahead, you will see the unmistakeable shape of Armchair Rock – or as some call it – the Devil's Armchair – looming. It really does look just like a huge armchair, all you need is a giant Neptune to sit in it, resting his feet in the sea.

Just by the rock is the most delicious little shingle cove with a lagoon of crystal-clear water at high tide, and the most extraordinary limestone formations which are variously like honeycomb, Gaudi buildings, or even skeletons or bones. The fact that they look a bit bone-like kind of makes sense, as the limestone is actually a fossilised coral reef. Locals like to come and spend time on this little beach, away from the crowds, and it's good for jumping and diving at high water.

As you pass Armchair Rock, you're starting the last leg of the swim. The amiable curve of Broadsands hoves into view, with its pretty

beach huts, but just before you get there you pass Crystal Cove on your right, a little suntrap in the late afternoon. It is so-called because the cliffs here contain crystalline calcite and rose quartz crystals. If you look carefully, you can see large chunks of the stuff in the rocks. It is the only place in the region where these crystals are found. The Victorians apparently found it fascinating, and turned up in their droves to see it, but also did some damage, with some visitors removing the crystal and selling it.

As you swim into Broadsands Bay, look out for the beautiful weathered sandstone cliff on your right, with fantastical holes and one particularly distinctive face. It calls to mind ancient temples carved into mountainsides, perhaps in Turkey or the Far East.

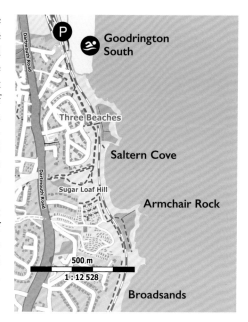

INFORMATION

SWIM ROUTE: From the beach at Goodrington, swim south with the coast on your right. Pass Saltern Cove, then Armchair Cove, and then Crystal Cove before arriving at Broadsands, where hopefully you will be collected, or will have left a car.

DISTANCE: I mile (2 if you swim there and back).

BEST TIDE STATE: High to mid tide.

SWIM HIGHLIGHT: Armchair Rock.

GET OUT POINTS: Armchair Cove.

POTENTIAL HAZARDS: The main danger is boats, so stay close to the shore. Wear a brightly coloured swim cap and use a tow float.

DOGS: Not allowed at Goodrington South and Broadsands beaches between I May and 30 September.

PARKING: Goodrington car park TQ4 6LP SX 891 596 what3words paints.cried.ruler; if you want to leave a car at Broadsands, the car park there is at TQ4 6HX SX 897 572 what3words: lakeside. picture.chops

PUBLIC TRANSPORT: The 23 bus stops on Dartmouth Road near Goodrington beach, and the 12 bus stops on Dartmouth Road near Goodrington Beach and also near Broadsands Beach.

REFRESHMENTS: South Sands beachside café at Goodrington serves hot drinks and snacks 07960 259152, The Venus Café at Broadsands serves hot food including local fish and burgers 07902 164293.

EASIER ACCESS: Goodrington Beach is close to the car park and is sandy so it is fairly easy to get in the water.

Swim 12

BROADSANDS BEACH TO ELBERRY COVE

A swim of contrasts, from the wide sandy bay at Broadsands, alongside a small limestone cliff, to the secluded beauty of Elberry Cove

As you sweep down the winding road to Broadsands, under the viaduct of the steam railway, there is a sense of grand expectation about what is to come. Unfortunately, the first sight is of the inevitable spread of concrete – the car park – but once at the beach it feels like a 1950s seaside idyll. Brightly painted beach huts line the prom, and every so often the steam train puffs by and whistles. Yet there is also a rural air, with soft green fields sloping up behind the beach; there is a working farm nearby. You can also see two of Brunel's lofty viaducts, which carry passengers of the Dartmouth Steam Railway between Paignton anf Kingswear.

Like many of the swims in Torbay, this is a journey from the slightly surburban feeling of a family 'bucket and spade' beach, to something rather wilder. The swim starts at the smooth red sands of Broadsands, littered with razor shells and cuttlefish bones; in fact, on a recent swim, we found a dead cuttlefish trailing its black ink with some distinct bite marks. Perhaps it had been chomped by a seal?

The red sand tells us that the beach dates from the Permian period, about 250 million years ago, when Torbay was a very hot desert. The swim can be done at any state of the tide, but be aware that when it's low the water is very shallow at Broadsands and you may have to wade for a bit. There are great views to the left across the Bay to Torquay and Thatcher Rock in the distance. Keep to the right of the beach, as you look to the sea, and start swimming along the coastline with the shore on your right.

Soon the landscape changes dramatically. Great crinkly rock formations spring up in outlandish, even grotesque, shapes, as though created by hippies on acid. It all feels a bit 'Lord of the Rings'. Here you are swimming past Devonian limestone, which started out life as corals growing in a tropical sea. The corals were made of calcium carbonate which gradually dissolved and became solid rock. In most areas of limestone, you would have no idea that it was once made of corals, but here, between Broadsands and Elberry, it is obvious. Despite the dissolution process, the erosion of the water has picked out the coral shapes. They are beautiful and are emphasised by the encrustation of barnacles. You really feel as though you are swimming alongside a coral reef.

Depending on the state of the tide, there will be channels to swim through and rocks to swim around. At low tide you can see, and enter, shortly after leaving Broadsands, a wonderful cavern which then leads through to an archway which leads you to a mini rocky beach. Its entrance is framed by elongated shapes that look like praying hands. The sanctified atmosphere does not continue though because, sticking right up in the middle of the cave is a large phallus-shaped rock. Not for nothing have we christened this place the "Rude Cave". Those of a sensitive disposition should not enter!

As you continue to swim, you will notice how the rocks are festooned with an amazing array of seaweed, in particular the red dulse which sways gently and is good to eat, even raw. More unusually though, look out for sea grass growing on the sandy bottom. As you get towards Elberry, the next cove along, you will see more and more of it, especially as the water gets clearer as you get nearer the cove.

The sea grass, which is not a seaweed but a flowering plant, is rare and protected, and home to two species of sea horse; the short snouted and spiny varieties. 'Meadows' of the grass extend out from Elberry Cove; the grass is important because it's the breeding ground for many marine species. For example, squid and cuttlefish lay their eggs on the grass. It's

vulnerable too, because it grows in shallow waters and so is at risk of damage from man. There are special buoys marking the sea grass meadows, so mariners know not to anchor there.

Half way between Broadsands and Elberry you pass Churston Point. The headland behind is part of the old Manor of Lord Churston, who gave the headland for the building of a golf course in 1890. Recently it has been rewilded and is a stunning place for a walk. If you look to your left, out and across towards Brixham harbour, you will see what looks like lines of black dots on the surface of the water in the distance. This is a mussel farm, the first in the country to grow these shellfish offshore. They are grown on ropes and are said to be much fatter and juicer because of the rich environment of the open sea. It's an interesting development in the fishing economy of Torbay.

Soon you will arrive at Elberry Cove, which may well take your breath away. The water here is crystal clear and the shingle beach is full of beautiful white and pink stones; on a sunny day the water is turquoise and it is reminiscent of the waters of a Greek island. As you swim over the sea grass, you may well see what

look like heart-shaped shells studding the seabed. It is fun to dive and try and pick them up, but you have to grab them very gently or they will shatter. These are not actually shells but the skeleton of a type of sea urchin called a sea potato. When the creature is alive it is covered with hairy spines that look a bit like fur. It lives in the sand and eats organic waste, so the presence of lots of them at Elberry is a sign of how clean the environment is here. There are also undersea freshwater springs in the area, which can be seen bubbling up through the sea on a calm day.

At the end of the cove, you will see an elegant ruin. This is known as Lord Churston's Bathing House and was purpose-built for seaside recreation. It is not known when it was actually built; some say the eighteenth, some say the nineteenth century. A fascinating paper published by the Devonshire Association in 1999 says the first definite evidence of its existence appeared in 1839, when it was mentioned in a survey for the Churston Parish tithe map. And a few decades later, in 1865 it was described on the Ordnance Survey map as a Bathing House.

It was originally thatched, and the ground floor was designed to flood, so as to provide a private bathing place for his lordship. There was a circular pool on the ground floor which, apparently, served as a hot tub. When the sea water filled up the pool it was then heated by

two boilers. One of the butlers had the unenviable task of coming down in advance from the manor house inland to light the fire for heating the copper.

Whether Lord Churston preferred to have a wonderful sweat in his hot tub followed by an invigorating dip in the sea outside, or vice versa, is open to debate. Perhaps he did both. The building was also used as a sort of upmarket beach hut for the Churston family; there was an upstairs room with furniture and fine china where they would take tea, which was no doubt lugged down from the manor house by retinues of servants.

Elberry Cove was a filming location for one of the final scenes in the 1964 film The System starring Oliver Reed and directed by Michael Winner. An outrageous beach party takes place here, while scenes were also filmed in the bathing house, which was far more intact at the time.

On the outside of the building, facing the sea, is some rather odd graffiti. Painted in huge neat white letters it says "No Numpty, One Way" with a large arrow. It may, perhaps, be some sort of message to the water-skiers who like to pursue their sport round here.

Talking of water-skiers, in the summer you will notice a line of yellow buoys cutting Elberry Cove in half. This is obviously a potential danger for us swimmers. The power boats that drag the skiers are allowed to drive

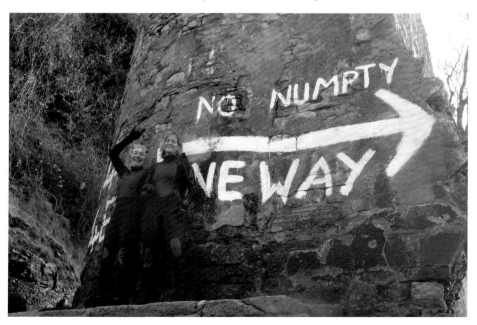

into the southern half of the cove, so do not swim in this area.

Elberry was one of Agatha Christie's favourite bathing spots; her holiday home at Greenway is not far away, and Elberry features in one of her novels, *The ABC Murders*, when Detective Hercule Poirot arrives at Churston station to investigate the murder of Sir Carmichael Clarke at the cove.

Poirot's assistant Hastings narrates the story as follows: 'We went down the lane. At the foot of it a path led between brambles and bracken down to the sea. Suddenly we came out on a grassy ridge overlooking the sea and a beach of glistening white stones. All round dark trees ran down to the sea. It was an enchanting spot – white, deep green – and sapphire blue. 'How beautiful!' I exclaimed. Clark turned to me eagerly. 'Isn't it? Why people want to go abroad to the Riviera when they've got this! I've wandered all over the world in my time and, honest to God, I've never seen anything as beautiful.'

We couldn't agree more. It's a beautiful and secluded gem and one of our favourite dipping spots around the Bay. You can swim back the way you came, or else it is a short walk back to Broadsands over the headland. Another way of doing the swim 'one way' is to change at Broadsands and walk in your swim stuff over to Elberry and swim back.

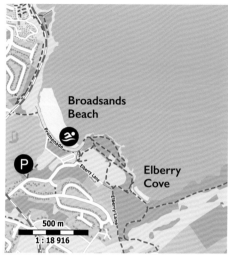

INFORMATION

SWIM ROUTE: From Broadsands Beach, swim out to sea with the shore on your right. At the mouth of the cove, turn right, and follow the coastline south, alongside the small limestone cliff. If it is low tide, look out for the Rude Cave shortly after leaving Broadsands. Carry on, admiring the gullies and channels, until you reach Elberry Cove. Either swim back the way you came or walk back over the golf course.

DISTANCE: 1 mile (there and back).

BEST TIDE STATE: Mid to high. It can also be done at low, when the "Rude Cave" is exposed.

SWIM HIGHLIGHT: Elberry Cove and Lord Churston's Bathing House

GET OUT POINTS: There are places between Broadsands and Elberry where you can climb out.

POTENTIAL HAZARDS: Be particularly alert for water skiers in power boats. They are permitted to ski into the southern half of Elberry Cove (where the Bathing House is). Do not swim in this half of the beach. (Get out and go and look at the Bathing House from the beach). Wear a brightly coloured swim cap and a tow float. Seals are also seen here. If one approaches, swim away calmly and quietly, without making sudden movements.

DOGS: Are allowed on Elberry Cove all year round; they are not allowed on the beach at

Broadsands between 1 May and 30 September.

PARKING: Broadsands car park TQ4 6HX SX 897 572. what3words: lakeside.picture.chops

PUBLIC TRANSPORT: The 12 bus stops by Broadsands Library, and it's a short walk down to the beach.

REFRESHMENTS: The K'ohana is situated right on Broadsands Beach, and serves drinks and snacks. 07780 990656. Churston Court is a historic pub and hotel dating back to Saxon times and has an open fire. 01803 842186.

EASIER ACCESS: Parking is very close to the beach, and access into the water (especially at high tide) is fairly easy.

FISHCOMBE COVE TO CHURSTON COVE

A swim between two coves in an exceptionally pretty part of Brixham; just look out for seals!

*I*n this swim you hardly feel you are in Torbay at all; no buildings are visible and the scene is virtually unchanged from a hundred years ago, as seen on old postcards. On a sunny day, the water is turquoise; it dances and sparkles in the light. It's like being in the Mediterranean, as you swim through the crystal-clear sea and past the idyllic woods, which are filled with twisted trees with carpets of flowers beneath.

Charles Gregory wrote a guide to Brixham in 1896. He spoke of the 'often motionless waters glittering in the sunshine of summer like a lake of molten silver' and went on, 'the sea, in Torbay, is actually often as blue as that of Naples, making a bright picture in conjunction with the ruddy rocks and rose-tinted sands along the sea shore.' He could well have been describing Fishcombe and Churston coves.

As you walk to Fishcombe from the parking area, you will pass the Brixham Battery Heritage Centre which is housed in an old artillery training hut which was used during World War II. Maintained by a dedicated crew of volunteers, it is open between March and October and is always worth a visit. It has lots of interesting artefacts, and even has a genuine WW2 Anderson Shelter you can enter.

The Battery - which refers to artillery weapons and the soldiers who operate them - played a major role in defending Torbay from enemy attack. Because of its position, this headland has always been an important defence post throughout history; the first records show it was used as a battery in 1586, in the war against the Spanish. Now it is a pleasant park and is the traditional vantage point for watching the annual Brixham Trawler Race.

It's a fairly steep walk down to the beach, which is small and pebbled. There is a fantastic café housed in a jolly hut painted in white and blue stripes like a deckchair. It's really community and environmentally orientated and they often organise fun charity events and talks. A number of great conservation organisations are associated with Fishcombe, including the Cove Discovery Project and the Seal Project (www.thesealproject.org). Wild Planet Trust have also installed boat moorings, designed to protect the fragile seagrass meadows found here.

To the right are some old concrete steps with a handrail that lead down into the water, just like in a swimming pool. And if it's a fine, still day, it feels just like a swimming pool too: gloriously blue and translucent. Apparently, in the old days, a bathing platform used to be anchored in deep water off the beach. As you look out to sea, your destination of Churston Cove is over to the left, beckoning you with its glorious pale shingle.

Be aware of the seals who are frequently seen around here. They are quite bold and may well come up to you while you are swimming. This has happened to us a couple of times. The important thing is to stay calm and do not make any sudden movements. Do not approach them either. They are extremely unlikely to hurt you, and are usually just curious. The good thing about this swimming route is that you can stay close to the coast and so if this does happen you can get out and watch them for a while.

For over a hundred years Fishcombe has played host to holidaymakers and pleasure seekers; the holiday camp above the beach (fortunately well hidden) started just before the Second World War as the Torbay Holiday Chalets and is still going strong today. Old photos show a packed beach; today it is rarely that busy which is great for swimmers but perhaps a sad sign of the decline of the British holiday.

The swim is best done at high water, as it is a rocky beach with painful pebbles. Start swimming along with the coast on your left. Pretty soon you might see a mini rock arch

which is only visible on a lower state of the tide. It is fun to swim through; the colour of the water intensifies as you approach; it then changes as you swim underneath; you emerge into what feels like a little 'room'. Keep going; there is lots to see below. There is a small sea grass bed here, but also lots of seaweed, like a little Bonsai garden underneath you. Lots of small fish dart around; the sea grass is a rich environment for them. There are bigger fish too, particularly wrasse which can be very brightly coloured.

You will pass a tiny beach, which is Barney's Cove. Up above and to your left is a small cliff, and above that is Marridge Wood, which is particularly beautiful in late spring when the garlic and bluebells are coming through. You'll soon come across a large rocky ledge, covered in barnacles, which drops away underwater like a cliff, and makes a perfect diving and jumping spot. Enjoy the feeling of plunging into the big blue. From here it's a short swim to Churston Cove, a very popular spot where people often camp overnight in good weather. The beach parties can and frequently do go on long into the night.

If you fancy it, it's fun to get out here and take the path in the middle of the beach into the woods. This is actually an ancient route to the old village of Churston. Apparently in Elizabethan times sea captains would arrive at the Cove and would go via an old underground passage to the Inn – now Churston Court – inland. The woods here are very pretty, but sadly in 2017 many of the trees had to be cut down, as they were infected. Around 5000 new trees were planted, which are now establishing well. You might see disused lime kilns, where limestone from the quarries nearby was burnt with coal to produce quicklime. This product was used as mortar for buildings, and also as fertiliser.

As you return to the beach you will see a long straight arm of cliff to the left, giving the cove a rectangular feel. It's like a natural jetty, which is probably why the beach used to be known as Churston Quay. Swim along here to

the end which is confusingly called Fishcombe Point. Here a large rock looms up like a seal's head. It surrounds a small inlet, revealed on a lower tide, that we have christened Mermaid's Pool. The water here is incredibly clear and there is a veritable underwater garden which is utterly hypnotic. There are particularly good specimens of tooth wrack and bladder wrack. You can get out and sit, like a mermaid, and gaze into the water watching the light play on the seaweed, and listening to the soft lapping

133

of the sea around you. It is beautiful.

After a short rest and pool watch, you can then get in again and swim around the corner to the left where you will soon come across a vast flat slab of rock, conveniently placed for lying down and basking in the sun. Perhaps it's somewhere the seal likes to stop? You can then climb back over the rocks to the Mermaid Pool. At the top of Fishcombe Point it is grassy and there is a rather poignant memorial there. It's one of those containers for flowers you get in cemeteries, but has a plaque which reads 'DAD, Charlie Buck. Diving was your passion, now diving is our love, now you watch us dive here, from heaven up above.' On our visit there were no flowers in the container but the message was still very poignant.

To get back to Fishcombe, you can either swim straight across from Fishcombe Point, or else retrace your strokes, going back via Churston Cove. Although now this is largely a place of recreation, these coves were places of industry in the past; both for smuggling and for shipbuilding. It seems hardly possible, but there were shipyards at both Churston and Fishcombe in the nineteenth century; very little is known about them, but we do know the one at Fishcombe was called Osbourne's.

On a summer's day, swimming through these tranquil waters, it is hard to imagine just how destructive the elements can be. But one tragic event here over a hundred years ago illustrates it well. The so -called Great Gale or Cyclone started on a January night with snow

and a strong wind which eventually became a hurricane, killing over a hundred people and wrecking boats between Brixham and Goodrington. Fishcombe and Churston were right on the hurricane's course, and Charles Gregory, in his Brixham guide of 1896, written thirty years later, described the scene:

'...the shore was one mass of wreckage and the remains of many seamen were found along the coast wrapped up in canvas...in Churston Cove a large ship went to pieces; of her crew of ten only four were saved. A schooner was at this spot actually carried by the sea right up onto a field above – the whole of her crew being thereby landed on terra firma.'

It's a chilling reminder of the power and changeability of the sea.

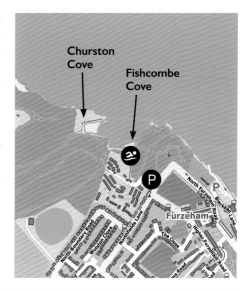

INFORMATION

SWIM ROUTE: From Fishcombe Cove, swim to the left, hugging the coast. Pass tiny Barney's Cove, and carry on to Churston Cove. Here you can get out and explore the beach, before carrying on along the left-hand side of the cove to the Mermaid Pool and Fishcombe Point. You can swim around Fishcombe Point and further along towards Elberry for as far as you like. Turn back when you feel like it and you can either go back the way you came or swim back directly from Fishcombe Point across to Fishcombe Cove.

DISTANCE: 0.3 miles.

BEST TIDE STATE: High to mid.

SWIM HIGHLIGHT:
Churston Cove.

GET OUT POINTS: Churston Cove, and various rocks along the route.

POTENTIAL HAZARDS: Seals are often in this part of Torbay. They can be curious, but are unlikely to hurt you. Stay calm and don't approach them or make any sudden movements. It's also popular with boaters in the summer, so wear a bright cap and a tow float.

DOGS: Are allowed all year round

PARKING: Free small car park on Fishcombe Road TQ5 8RU SX 920 567 what3 words: through. plank.envisage.

PUBLIC TRANSPORT: The 12 bus stops in the centre of Brixham from where it is a 10-15 minute walk. The local Brixham 17 bus stops on Northfield Lane which is a few minutes walk from Fishcombe Cove.

REFRESHMENTS: the Fishcombe Cove Café, which is open between Easter and November, is right on the beach and serves great food as well as putting on live music. fishcombecovecafe@gmail.com Simply Fish in the centre of Brixham is a friendly restaurant specialising in seafood which also does takeaway. 01803 859585.

THE BREAKWATER TO BERRY HEAD SWIM

A fascinating route from Brixham's breakwater, past its famous lido, and out towards the very southernmost tip of the Bay

The colourful surf shack-style Breakwater Bistro makes a great meeting point for a swim from the bleached pebbles of Breakwater Beach, past Shoalstone Point and towards the elegant Berry Head Hotel. The café also has a really useful webcam so you can check out weather and sea conditions. You can take in some great views right across the Bay to Torquay from the café terrace while you enjoy some pre-swim nourishment. You'll also get a fantastic look at the breakwater itself, an impressive structure built to protect the port from harsh easterly gales and to provide safe anchorage.

If you think that projects take a long time to come to fruition these days, the breakwater took 69 years and quite literally a lifetime to complete. Money twice ran out for the huge public project and the breakwater wasn't actually finished until 1912, but we are sure that the people of Brixham appreciate this protective arm that safely hugs the boats within. It also makes an amazing half a mile walk, especially at dusk, with spectacular views out across the Bay and back towards Brixham itself.

The perfect time to swim is the bottom half of the tide, ideally about two hours after low water, when an amazing array of rock sculptures can be viewed, like a flooded mini–Monument Valley. This will enable you to see the features of interest on the way out, and then, as you swim back, the tide will be coming back in. It's definitely worth wearing some protective footwear, as clambering opportunities abound.

You will notice a rather grand, gothic-looking house which towers over the beach, complete with a 'widow's walk' at the top. It is called Wolborough House, and was built in 1910 by Charles Hellier, who owned a fleet of fishing trawlers. It is highly ornate, and apparently Italian craftsmen were brought over to create the marble frieze work on the outside of the building. It has a stained-glass window with local historical scenes, including the arrival of William of Orange. The house is available for holiday lets.

The swim route takes you east, starting on the right-hand side of the beach (looking out to sea). Begin by scrambling over the long cement structure and the natural wall of rocks bordering the beach (or else you can swim around) and look out for a tiny natural pool left as the tide retreats. It would make the ideal spot for teaching nymphs, imps, fairies or very small mermaids to swim.

You may notice a barnacle-encrusted set of steps from the wall going down to the water, like some forgotten 1970s prog-rock album cover. We like to think they were once used by the residents of Wolborough House as their private route into the sea, but sadly the wall is now bricked up and the steps are a tantalising reminder of the Bay's former golden age of swimming.

This area between Breakwater Beach and Shoalstone Pool is known locally as Ladybird Cove. No one seems to know why. You will pass a series of six pillar-like rocks, like giant's teeth, which are fun to navigate a winding path around. You'll also notice that the swim is the one of the most urban of those included in the book, with an interesting collection of buildings gazing out to sea from their domineering position above you. Small abandoned wartime warehouses stand side by side with holiday lets and charming former coast-guard cottages.

Below the houses, at the bottom of the rock faces, you'll see signs of man's battle with nature, with generous amounts of cement and hundreds of sandbags used to fortify the cliffs. The natural and the man-made have

fused together over the decades to create a fascinating palette of colours and textures. See if you can spot a pile of sandbags that time and tide has sculpted into what resembles a font or a shrine to some legendary god of the sea.

As you continue, you'll be able to see some impressive walls towering above you and the underside of the two small bridges which form part of the coast path above. Look out for a rock shaped like a petrified cacti below the cliffs, and a curious collection of oddly shaped rocks that, with a little imagination, look like the ruins of some ancient civilisation inhabited by incredible natural statues of gods and monsters.

Swim on following the curve of the wall above, and a little beach we have dubbed Cormorant Cove appears. We spotted several of these beautiful seabirds here, drying on the rocks. Swim past the cove on your right and you'll approach a startling rectangle of rock that looks like it is embedded with hundreds of skulls, not unlike the macabre catacombs in Paris. The heads seem to be forever frozen with expressions of pain and torment, like a Wailing Wall and a tribute to all those lost at sea.

As you continue to swim through the crystal-clear waters, more rocks with the faces of strange creatures appear. It's a curious geological effect and due to the number of

rocks and the various routes you can swim, we decided to name this area the Monster Maze. The honeycombed look of the rocks caused one of our group, Rachel, to describe them as "marine Crunchie Bars" – although we suspect they are not quite as palatable as the popular confectionery.

As you swim past the outside walls of Shoalstone Pool, why not have a scramble up the rocks to look at this much-loved seawater swimming pool, and maybe even have a dip. This famous lido – which is 53 metres long - began life as a natural rock pool, which is why it has a somewhat curious shape. In 1896, two walls were built around some rocks to retain water and allow bathing whatever the state of the tide. In 1926, further improvements were made, including the removal of lots of bedrock, creating a shallow and a deep end with twice the depth of the original.

The Brixham Swimming and Lifesaving Society was formed here in 1928, aimed at teaching the town's children to swim. One of those children was Bryan Watkins, the father of Dylan Watkins, a local GP.

Following the Second World War, the start of the swimming season used to be marked by a local lady called Minnie Bowman jumping off the old diving board, wrapped in a Union Jack flag. A tradition that surely needs to be revived! A storm severely damaged the pool in 1979 and the council considered closing it. However, such was the strength of public opinion, they found the money to repair the pool and to build the wall along the sea edge you are now peering over. In 2022, a huge

shoal of fish became trapped in the pool and died over night due to a lack of oxygen. It took a huge public effort to clear up the thousands of dead fish and dispose of them properly.

It seems that every year funding issues threaten to close the pool, but thanks to the efforts of local people this has not happened. The pool is run by a community interest company, and volunteers give up many hours of their time repairing the pool and painting it with donated trawler and lifeboat paint, as well as taking on the more complicated jobs of running the attraction safely and securing grants.

Back in the water, you get a wonderful view of the Berry Head Hotel from the sea. It was originally built in 1805 as a military hospital during the Napoleonic wars. Ironically, Napoleon himself would have been treated to a similarly unique look at this imposing cliff top building in 1815 following his defeat at Waterloo. He was held in a British warship off Berry Head, before spending the rest of his days in exile on the isle of St Helena. On first seeing Torbay he is quoted as saying "enfin, voila un beau pays!" (finally, here is a beautiful country!), likening the Bay to Porto Ferraio in Elba.

Just before you reach the hotel, a secret pebble beach appears, with some truly impressive homes keeping tight lipped about the secluded beauty at the bottom of their gardens. One of the houses is called Berry Head Rocks, which would also make a rather good name for a music festival. It's cleverly designed so it can't be seen from the road behind, perfectly blending in with the natural environment.

Following the Napoleonic Wars, the Berry Head Hotel fell into disrepair for 18 years, before becoming the vicarage of the Rev Henry Francis Lyte, who not only served the needs of his flock at All Saints Church, but also raised money to provide food and clothing for the poor, opened a school for local children and reduced the adult illiteracy rate in the town. He also wrote over 300 hymns and poems, including Abide With Me, one of the most famous hymns ever written. The church now rings out three of his hymns daily, including Abide With Me at 8pm as "fast falls the eventide." The house was turned into a hotel in 1949.

There are some huge rocks at the base of the hotel, ideal for drying off in the sunshine and exploring. You'll spot some great natural seawater swimming pools which are sure to have attracted hotel guests over the years, while with a little bit of hunting you'll find what looks like a small metal cross embedded in the rocks. It has no inscription, but it is nice to think of it perhaps as a tribute to the vicar who lived here for so many years.

Now you have the choice of swimming back, or walking up the steps to the hotel and taking the road and path back. Or why not pop into the hotel in your wetsuit James Bond-style first and order a nice refreshing drink. On the rocks, obviously. We dare you!

SWIM ROUTE: From Breakwater Beach, swim around to the right (or else clamber over the rocks), with the shore on your right. Follow the coastline around past Shoalstone Pool (where you can stop and have a dip if you fancy) and then continue on until you are by the Berry Head Hotel. Swim back the way you came (or you can get out and walk back).

DISTANCE: 0.6 miles (there and back).

BEST TIDE STATE: Low to mid.

SWIM HIGHLIGHT: Shoalstone Pool

GET OUT POINTS: Shoalstone Pool, shore near Berry Head Hotel.

POTENTIAL HAZARDS: It is quite rocky so swim shoes are advised. The swim is close to the shore so there aren't usually too many boats to worry about. It's advisable to wear a bright swim cap and a tow float.

DOGS: Not allowed on Breakwater Beach between 1 May and 30 September.

PARKING: Breakwater car park TQ5 9AF SX931 566 what3words roughest.travels.disco

PUBLIC TRANSPORT: The 12 bus stops in the centre of Brixham from where it is a 10-minute walk. The local Brixham 17 bus stops at Breakwater Beach.

REFRESHMENTS: The Breakwater Bistro is right on the beach and serves seafood, burgers and waffles. 01803 856738. Shoals Restaurant has a great position by the lido and serves a range of seafood 01803 854874.

EASIER ACCESS: The car park at Breakwater Beach is right next to the water, with only a couple of steps down to the beach.

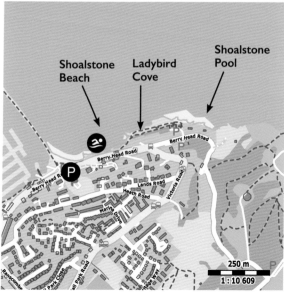

143

Swim 15

ST MARY'S BAY
TO DURL ROCK

An exciting swim adventure in one of the wildest
corners of the Bay, visiting an unusual rock formation

St Mary's Bay in Brixham is a spectacular, unspoilt beach whose beauty has enchanted everyone from Iron Age man to the Romans and World War II soldiers. It's also been captured for prosperity in thousands of faded Polaroid photos taken by holiday makers who flocked to the many holiday camps which overlooked the beauty spot in the 1960s, 70s and 80s.

It's not just tourists who have made the pilgrimage to the town over the centuries, but the those drawn to a legendary well, about a mile inland from St Mary's Bay. During the eighteenth and early nineteenth centuries, people came from all over the world to visit The Laywell Spring. It had a famous power of "ebbing and flowing like the tide, several times an hour" and a shrine was built, complete with stone deities. Sadly, the spring is now lost. However, a statue from the shrine washed downstream and survived. It can still be seen in St Mary's Church. And who needs a healing stream when we have the magical waters of the English Channel?

Walking down towards the beach from the car park you'll cross the South West Coast Path. This stretch from Berry Head to your left, curving around to Sharkham Point to the right was originally the Coastguard Walk and according to the *Book of Brixham* by Frank Pearce, this was a popular area with smugglers over the centuries. No doubt the ghosts of the coastguards – and perhaps also the smugglers – patrol this path to this day.

As you walk down the steep steps to the beach, you'll be able to spot the soft, middle Devonian shales which have eroded away to form what was once called "Mudstone Bay." These slate-like shales and the rich geology of the area, including many fossils found on the beach, have contributed to this stretch of coastline being declared a Site of Special Scientific Interest (SSSI) and an Area of Outstanding Natural Beauty.

The name of the beach was almost certainly changed to the more romantic sounding St Mary's Bay as more tourists began to arrive in town. The beach itself is a geologist's dream, boasting both sandy stretches and a huge colourful array of different pebbles, hinting at the mining history of the area. Iron ore was mined at Sharkham Point, limestone at Berry Head and ochre in Furzeham. The latter was used to produce a ground-breaking rust-resistant red paint (invented in Brixham in 1845) which was hugely important in the industrial revolution. It was even painted on the sails of trawlers; hence the song "Red Sails in the Sunset" said to have been written about the iconic Brixham fishing fleet.

The swim starts at the northern end of the beach, on the left as you look out to sea. We strongly advise swimming this route on a neap tide at slack water (an hour either side of high or low tide), to avoid a current which can develop and take you out into the centre of the Bay. There is more about understanding tides in the introduction, and more details on this particular current in the information box.

Walking along the shore, you will see plenty of clues to the relentless and unapologetic power of nature. Not only will you find huge breccia boulders (nature's cement made from washed away desert sands, packed with colourful stones collected along the way), but man-made cement blocks as well. You might see sections of red brick walls lying about, pulled apart by tides and time, perhaps the remains of the Victorian cafe or the former lifeboat station that once operated from the beach in the 1800s.

As you enter the water, look out for the seals who are often spotted in this area, while if you are really lucky you may even spot pods

of bottlenose dolphins, harbour porpoises and basking sharks swimming near the shore.

On a sunny day it's truly spectacular swimming below these towering cliffs, whose sculpted walls tells the story of millions of years of dramatic geological movements. The colour of the sea also takes on an incredibly intense jade hue, enhanced by the red of the sandstone above. You'll also no doubt spot people walking along the coast path above - don't fret, you've still got the best view!

Soon you'll swim past a giant rock that the most curious of wild swimmers won't be able to resist climbing out onto. However, be warned, those with a low pong threshold might want to avoid this, as the rock is popular with cormorants and other sea birds, and absolutely reeks of guano. Next, swim towards the centre of the pair of rocks we have dubbed "twin peaks" for obvious reasons and you'll be able to see the goal of Durl Rock in the distance.

The cliffs get more fascinating as you swim. There are areas of moss that have been fossilised into the rocks and resemble faces. One time along here we thought we could see the face of a gorilla (we may have drunk too much salt water by this point). Looking towards your destination you might spot a kink of light winking through a natural hole in the cliffs at Durl Point, while Durl Rock itself seems to

resemble a somnolent swimmer, floating on their back with their toes pointed skywards.

The rock is popular with both anglers and scuba divers, thanks to the incredibly rich marine life found below the surface at this stunning spot. Swim around the pointed end of the rock and it's fun to scramble up out of the sea before plunging back into the deep cool waters. As you round Durl Rock, you'll be able to see the huge promontory of Berry Head in the distance.

The headland was first used as a defensive stronghold by Iron Age man, and later used by the Romans before the present forts were built upon the former strongholds during the Napoleonic wars, to protect the shores from the threat of French invasion. It's home to over 500 species of plants, including rare orchids, and a host of wildlife including 200 species of birds and the largest guillemot colony on the South Coast. These birds are known by locals as the "Brixham Penguins", although perhaps "Brixham Lemmings" would be a better nickname. Each year, over a couple of nights coinciding with the summer solstice, hundreds of chicks throw themselves from the cliffs with suicidal vigour. As Nick Pannell explains in his book Tor Bay - The History and wildlife of Torbay's dramatic shoreline (1998):

"It's a dramatic event. The chicks wait till dusk and then, responding to some unknown signal, throw themselves from the ledges, featherless wings flapping to no effect. Many actually collide with the rock face as they fall

but survive to join their parents in the rising swell. They continue to be nurtured by their parents for many weeks."

As you continue round Durl Rock, the sea takes on a deeper and more intense colour and you'll reach a large flat natural platform, ideal for a rest before the return journey. Off to your right you'll be able to take in the beauty of two islets, the nearer Mew Stone and the distant Cod Rock. To your left, several caves and coves can be spotted beneath the cliffs of Berry Head.

At this point, it's time to turn around and start swimming back. On your way say "Hi-De-Hi!" to the holiday park up on the hill. The Riviera Bay Holiday Park was formally known as The St Mary's Bay Camp and was one of five Pontins in the area back in the twentieth century. All of the others have now been demolished, with new houses being built in their place.

You can imagine the laughter and music spilling over the cliffs and drifting out to sea, back in the golden era of the Great British Holiday. Back then the Barnacle Club would have been packed with people enjoying the fun and games on offer, including Miss Pontins, Elegant Grandmother, Miss Model Girl and the, erm, "Eligible Escort". Many people have a fondness for these bygone days when families would save up all year for their annual all-inclusive chalet holiday on the

English Riviera, lured by the slogan, 'All your want-ins at Pontin's.'

With many of the swims in this book, it's easy to feel the dull ache of nostalgia for times sadly passed. But the knowledge that there are still miles of unspoiled places to discover and dozens of remarkable places to escape the pressures and accelerations of modern life, more than compensates for any brief moments of melancholy. After all, your explorations provide unique access to some wonderful sights only a fraction of people will ever get to experience. So, chin up, it's time for a well-deserved hot chocolate and to reminisce about the last amazing hour of your life. And to plan your next swim adventure.

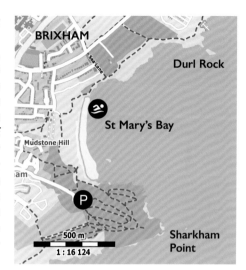

INFORMATION

SWIM ROUTE: From the northern end of St Mary's Bay, swim out beside the shore, with the cliffs on your left. Continue to hug the coastline until you reach the long arm of Durl Rock. You can swim a little further, or else turn around and swim back the way you came.

DISTANCE: 1.2 miles.

BEST TIDE STATE: You need to swim on a neap tide at slack water, an hour either side of high or low tide. This is because of a current. (See hazards below).

SWIM HIGHLIGHT: Durl Rock.

GET OUT POINTS: None.

POTENTIAL HAZARDS: There is a current about 0.4 miles into the swim, before you reach Durl Rock,

which can pull you out, away from the coast, into the middle of the bay. Keep close to the shore, and also swim at slack water so the water movement is at its quietest. You are unlikely to come into contact with boats, but it is still a good idea to wear a brightly coloured swim cap and a tow float. Seals are also possible in this area; if you see one do not approach it but swim away from it, avoiding sudden movements.

DOGS: Are allowed all year round.

PARKING: Sharpham Point car park TQ5 9GQ, SX 932 547 what3words: charm.pits.albatross

PUBLIC TRANSPORT: The local 17 bus calls at the Riviera Holiday Park from where you can walk to

the coast path and thence to the beach; the 12 bus calls in the centre of town from where St Mary's Bay is a 20-minute walk.

REFRESHMENTS: The Bell Inn in nearby Higher Brixham serves pub grub and Sunday roasts 01803 851815. The Curious Kitchen in the centre of town serves falafels and wraps as well as brioche baps 01803 854816. We love the Wine Loft just above the harbour where you can enjoy wines complimented by delicious tapas.

EASIER ACCESS: Unfortunately, the beach is not that accessible. There is a steep walk down from the car park, and then a lot of steps down to the beach.

Health, Safety and Responsibility

Like any water-based activity, sea swimming and coastal exploration has risks and can be dangerous and these are described more fully inside. Few of the locations featured in this book have lifeguards and all are prone to tidal immersion, currents and sea-state changes. While the author and publisher have gone to great lengths to ensure the accuracy of the information herein they will not be held legally or financially responsible for any accident, injury, loss or inconvenience sustained as a result of the information or advice contained in this book. Swimming, jumping, diving, scrambling or any other activities at any of these locations is entirely at your own risk.

Copyright

This edition published in the United Kingdom in 2023 by Wild Things Publishing Ltd. ISBN 9781910636411. Text copyright © 2023 Matt Newbury & Sophie Pierce. The moral rights of the author have been asserted. All rights reserved.

Cover photo:
Dan Bolt
Design and layout:
Gary Nickolls
Proofreading:
Michael Lee
Mapping:
Open Street Map

Published by:
Wild Things Publishing Ltd
Bath, BA2 7WG,
wildthingspublishing.com
hello@wildthingspublishing.com

Acknowledgements

Special thanks to Dan Bolt for his beautiful photographs, and to Ken Stapleton who took us out in his boat, enabling Dan to take the images. Another person who was crucial in the making of this book was Jim Wills, a renowned local historian who shared so much of his knowledge, as well as his books and old photographs. Sadly, both these dear men are no longer with us; Jim died in 2020, and Ken in 2021. Both are much missed. Thank you to Mike Holgate for lending the photo of Tack Collings. We are grateful to Hayley Barnard, Charlotte Gustar, Allan Macfadyen, Sally Morgan, Andrew Oliver, Chris Popham and Rosie Spooner for additional photography. We would also like to thank Anna Allen and Melanie Border who helped us with the text. Thank you

also to Daniel Start from Wild Things Publishing, who helped us give this book a new lease of life. Thank you to all the wonderful swimmers in Devon who have swum with us and supported the project and thanks to "you" for buying a copy! And last of all thanks to our partners Aaron and Alex who have put up with innumerable 'Gone Swimming' notes on the kitchen table.

Photo credits

All images by Matt Newbury, Sophie Pierce and Aaron Kitts, apart from P2, 6, 10, 12, 17 bottom, 18, 22, 25, 28, 30, 31, 32, 33, 34, 40, 41, 42, 43, 44 Dan Bolt, P46 Charlotte Gustar, P48 Allan Macfadyen, P50 top Sally Morgan, P50 bottom Lynne Roper, P53 Sally Morgan, P56 Andrew Oliver, P59 Amanda Bluglass, P62, P65 bottom, P68, P71 Dan Bolt, P89, P96 Rosie Spooner, P100 Charlotte Gustar, P106, P108 Dan Bolt, P110 Hayley Barnard, P112 Dan Bolt, P124 Miriam Aston-Hetherington, P130 Rosie Spooner, P132 top Chris Popham, bottom Dan Bolt, P149, P150 Chris Popham, P152 Dan Bolt.

Other books from Wild Things